AMAZON
PEACOCK BASS
FISHING

Top Tactics for Top Locations

by Larry Larsen

Eight-Time World Record Holder and
1999 Inductee in Fishing Hall of Fame

Larsen's Outdoor Publishing
www.peacockbassassociation.com
www.larsenoutdoors.com

This Book Courtesy of:

Copyright (c) 2004 by Larry Larsen

Publisher's Cataloging in Publication

Larsen, Larry.
Amazon Peacock Bass Fishing - Top Tactics for Top Locations!
by Larry Larsen.

p. cm.
Includes index.
ISBN 0-936513-53-5

1. Bass fishing. 2. Peacock bass. I. Title. II. Title: Amazon
peacock bass fishing.

SH681.L37 2003799.1'78

ISBN 0-936513-53-5
Library of Congress Control Number: 2003096383

Published by:
LARSEN'S OUTDOOR PUBLISHING
2640 Elizabeth Place, Lakeland, FL 33813
www.peacockbassassociation.com
www.larsenoutdoors.com

PRINTED IN THE UNITED STATES OF AMERICA

1 2 3 4 5 6 7 8 9 10

LIBRARY ANNOTATION

Title: Amazon Peacock Bass Fishing

Author: Larry Larsen
Publisher: Larsen's Outdoor Publishing
Copyright: 2004

Sports & Recreation
Fishing
799.1

LCCN: 2003096383
ISBN: 0-936513-53-5

ADULT SMALL PRESS

From a Fishing Hall of Fame Legendary Angler and outdoors journalist, "Amazon Peacock Bass Fishing" focuses on catching America's greatest gamefish, the peacock bass. It offers tips on where, when and how to catch the exciting fish. Special features include productive tactics for the best locations in South America, tackle considerations, and secrets to catch larger and more peacock bass.

192 pages
Paperbound/Casebound

Table of Contents
Index
B&W Illustrations
Photographs

** Author Credentials **
He's America's most widely-read bass fishing writer and author. More than 2,000 of Larsen's articles have appeared in magazines, including Outdoor Life, Florida Sportsman, Sports Afield, Bassin' and Field & Stream. He was inducted into the Fishing Hall of Fame in 1999. Larsen has authored 20 books on largemouth and peacock bass fishing and contributed chapters to another ten.

DEDICATION

This book is dedicated to the members of the Peacock Bass Association (www.peacockbassassociation.com) who have helped to make PBA one of the most informative, successful associations spanning several countries. The avid peacock bass angler who is an individual member of PBA has given his/her trust to the association to keep them informed on the latest techniques, destinations and activities associated with this popular game fish. PBA's Supporting Members have actively improved their operations, products and services and grown professionally to provide a growing group of enthusiasts with productive operations/ facilities and excellent gear. This book is sincerely dedicated to all who pursue the world's most exciting freshwater sportfish!

And to my wife, Lilliam, who patiently puts up with my extended absences as I travel overseas to continue my photography and writing research on this exciting fishery and the fastest-growing sport in fishing.

ACKNOWLEDGMENTS

I would like to thank my friends in the outdoor travel industry, those tour operators, trip outfitters and tourism people that offer some of the most exciting, adventuresome opportunities in the world. A list of many of the helpful contacts who provided assistance and advice to make this effort comprehensive and interesting would have to include: Don Cutter, Peacock Bass Trips.Com, Phil Marsteller and Jim Kern, Amazon Tours, Scott Swanson, FishQuest, Wellington Melo and Ronaldo Gumiero, Xeriuini River Lodge, J.W. Smith, Rod & Gun Resources, Luis Brown, River Plate Outfitters, Lewis Cunningham, Reel It Up, Scott Ruprecht, Sportfishing Worldwide, Flavio Ferreira and Ian Sulocki, High Hook Fishing Tours, Iomar Oliveria, Voyager, Reinaldo Tonete, Nexus, Jan Wilt, Royal Amazon Lodge, C. Frederico Bais, Unini River Fishing Adventure, Claudomiro Gomes, Belo Monte Fishing Lodge, and Jesus Jacotte, Amazonas Peacock Bass Safari.

I also want to acknowledge the support of all the members, both Individual and Supporting, of the Peacock Bass Association. Thanks to all who share a love for the fish and who have a sincere desire to make PBA a force in the small, yet fast-growing industry. Your support enables PBA to focus on goals of conservation, knowledge and continual enjoyment to the world's greatest fish.

Finally, I want to thank my good friend Phil Jensen, owner of Luhr-Jensen Lures for his support in helping to sponsor this book. The company's support of peacock bass fishing has been long-standing in the development and production of more productive peacock lures than any other lure manufacturer. Luhr-Jensen has been a leader in the field of peacock bass tackle, and I welcome their support of my efforts in spreading knowledge about the great Amazon peacock bass fishing.

PREFACE

The focus of this book, "Amazon Peacock Bass Fishing" is to reveal some of the very best tactics to use in the very best waters offering the extraordinary peacock bass. In the Introduction, I examine the magnificent Amazon River and explain why it is unlike any other river in the world. You'll learn about the differences in the tributaries, why some are much better than others for peacock bass fishing, and you'll even learn some facts about the flora and fauna in the Basin.

This book takes a look at the world's most exciting fish, the peacock bass, and easily lays out the reasons for such admiration by the avid anglers that visit their native range: the Amazon Basin. The number of angling trips to the Amazon for peacock bass is greatly increasing each year as the fish continues rapid growth in popularity. While the chapters are titled based on a specific experience at a location in the Basin or the Operation that handled the trip, the most effective tactics and techniques are presented.

"Amazon Peacock Bass Fishing" is a valuable reference source with numerous strategies in each chapter to fool peacock bass. You'll learn tactics for "fry balls", "piranha bursts", post-rain, shallow and clear waters, "dolphin encounters", large lagoons, sandbar drops, walk-ins, "teener" schoolers, sight fishing, laydowns, storms, channels, irregular shorelines, topwater trolling, mid-lagoon haunts, "team" fishing, river bars and pools, "fly-outs" and flood stage waters. You'll also learn about lure modifications, lure cadence and rhythm, top bait colors and patterns, size selection of the lures, and many other tackle tips that will increase your productivity!

The "top tactics" at the top locations will work at most other locations, so the reader should understand the wealth of information that is presented in each and every chapter. He or she should be able to find many new, productive ways to catch giant peacock bass. Detailed illustrations and numerous photos highlight the most productive patterns.

This is a "where-to/how-to" book designed to help you catch more peacock bass everywhere.

I have attempted to provide readers with an honest overview of these opportunities in the Amazon, based on more than 50 weeks' worth of trips to the region in search of the giant peacock bass. All but the last chapter in this comprehensive book focuses on geographic areas in the Amazon that almost always produce good peacock bass fishing during the right water conditions. The last chapter discusses the world's only organization evolving around the fish, the fishery and those who love it.

Readers will discover several interesting and informative appendices, including detailed information on the first three books in this series, "Peacock Bass Explosions", "Peacock Bass & Other Fierce Exotics" and "Peacock Bass Addiction". There is also a World Peacock Bass Directory Contact List, courtesy of the Peacock Bass Association, which identifies most all of the world's major agents, operators and outfitters of peacock bass trips. You'll also find the contact information of major product manufacturers and services that cater to the avid peacock bass angler. You'll also find an Outdoor Resource Directory listing many products, books, etc. of interest to peacock bass chasers.

CONTENTS

The author has been featured in many magazines and promotional ads. Larry has sold more articles and photos of peacock bass than all other writers combined to numerous magazines, including *Sports Afield, Outdoor Life* and *Florida Sportsman,* as well as to newspapers, brochures and internet sites.

ABOUT THE AUTHOR

Larry Larsen travels to the Amazon in search of peacock bass more than any other writer/angler. While catching more than his share of the fish, he has studied the successful tactics that allow him to catch more large peacock bass than the majority of avid anglers. He focuses on the giants, which he calls "teeners" - those fish that weigh 13 pounds or more.

Over a period of 52 trips to South America, he has released 1,650 peacock weighing over ten pounds, including 480 "teeners", and 17 over 20 pounds. He continues his quest for the record-breaker 27-pound peacock!

Each trip adds to his "teener" total. For example, on his last trip to the Brazilian Amazon, his group of six anglers caught 40 "teeners" during the week. Larry caught 25 of them. Does he fish different waters or use a different scale? No. Everyone in the group changed fishing partners and guides each day, and the scales in each boat were IGFA certified. In this, his fourth comprehensive book in the series, Larsen shares the best methods for the top locations in the Amazon.

Larsen, a 1999 "Legendary Angler" inductee in the Fresh Water Fishing Hall of Fame, is a frequent contributor on both largemouth and peacock bass subjects to major outdoor magazines, including *Sports Afield, Field & Stream, Bassin'* and *Florida Sportsman.* He was Florida Editor for Outdoor Life for 14 years and is Editor-In-Chief of Larsen's Adventure Travel Magazine at www.larsenoutdoors.com. His photography and articles have appeared in more than 2,000 magazines.

For more than 18 years, the Lakeland, Florida outdoorsman has also authored and published books on fishing. He has written and published 19 freshwater fishing titles and contributed chapters to another 11. His works include the award-winning 9-volume Bass Series Library, the 3-volume Bass Waters Series. Larsen has authored three previous volumes of the Peacock Bass Series, the contents of which are outlined in the Appendix. His "Peacock Bass Explosions!" book has been translated into Portuguese and is sold throughout Brazil. With this fourth book and a soon-to-be-released video, "Masters' Secrets to Peacock Bass Fishing,"

Larry continues to be the foremost authority on peacock bass fishing in South America.

He most recently formed the Peacock Bass Association (www.peacockbassassociation.com) in an effort to unite all avid peacock anglers and the destinations which specialize in this unique fishery. This successful effort has generated increased momentum into the conservation and professionalism of this industry worldwide.

It is improbable that readers would not learn something from Larry's knowledge and experience with peacock bass. There are no journalists more qualified or knowledgeable about such waters. In fact, only a couple of anglers in the world have fished as many areas and caught as many giant peacock bass as Larry. Those who study these pages will expand their knowledge of the addiction that is called "peacock bass fishing."

The author/angler intensely studies all aspects of a fishing topic before writing about it. His works detail the proven fish locating and catching techniques. Larsen has worked with several tackle companies on lure development, drawing on his many years of fishing experience and an engineering background. He has fished bass extensively for more than 38 years, and for peacock bass more than 14 years.

Larsen has been the featured guest of numerous radio and television shows and has produced and hosted the video "Lowrance Electronics' Advanced Bass Fishing Tactics with Larry Larsen". He has presented numerous seminars and demonstrations on freshwater angling techniques at fishing expos in the Southeast U.S. and in South America. He has developed fishing techniques software and CD-ROM projects and has produced fishing information/illustration for more than 30 internet sites.

Larsen is also President of Larsen's Outdoor Publishing (www.larsenoutdoors.com), publishing a variety of outdoor titles, and a member of the Outdoor Writers Association of America (OWAA), the Southeastern Outdoor Press Association (SEOPA), and the Florida Outdoor Writers Association (FOWA).

INTRODUCTION

The Mysterious and Mighty Amazon

The Amazon is unlike any other river in the world. In the past 10 years, I've spent about 360 days on it chasing its euphoric bounty, the "tucunare" or peacock bass, as known by most. A love of the greatest fish in the world led me to their native range: the Amazon Basin. The Basin contains one-third of the world's remaining rainforest and drains an area two-thirds the size of the United States. In fact, over 40% of the rainfall over South America drains into the Basin.

In Brazil alone, the Basin encompasses 75% of the country geographically, including the states of Mato Grosso, Amazonas, Para, Tocantins, Goias and a couple of smaller ones. The vast Amazon River is 4,000 miles long and has over 7,000 tributaries, which extend throughout the northern two thirds of Brazil into the southern part of Venezuela and throughout the eastern parts of Peru, Colombia and

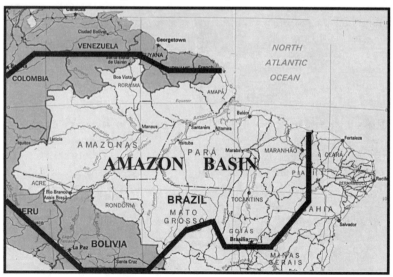

Bolivia. It averages three miles wide, and sometimes as much as six miles wide, with an average depth of around 300 feet!

Half of the 20 largest rivers in the world are in the Amazon Basin. Between one and six additional tributaries of the Amazon are larger than the Mississippi, according to some sources. The Amazon River itself may rise up to 60 feet between the rainy and dry season, and it can inundate vast areas of up to 60 miles from the main channel during the wet season. At the mouth of the river during the wet season, it is more than 200 miles wide!

Fortunately, the Amazon Basin, which basically surrounds the equator over its length, is not in the most populous part of the countries. While the mighty Amazon is a "boat" freeway for a few million people that subsist in the rain forest, its less-crowded tributaries are also home to 40 or more sportfishing operations that target peacock bass. In fact, the World Peacock Bass Directory at www.peacockbassassociation.com lists all of the significant fishing operations selling fishing tours in the Amazon region.

An Honorable Discharge

While the Nile is longer, the Amazon's discharge is 60 times more than the Nile's and in fact, is more than the next eight largest rivers in the world combined! To put the discharge in further perspective, the Amazon contributes 20%, or one-fifth, of all freshwater to the world's oceans. The volume of the Amazon River alone is so enormous that, in just 28 seconds, the river is capable of furnishing a liter of water to every inhabitant on the planet Earth!

Let's consider a shorter time period of just one second. Each second, the river discharges between 100,000 and 200,000 cubic meters of water (averaging 175,000 cubic meters) which weigh between 100,000 and 200,000 tons! In one second, it discharges enough water to supply a city of 14 million people for four years!

The Tributaries – Black, Clear & White Waters

The tributaries of the Amazon vary drastically. Some stretch for hundreds and hundreds of miles while others are relatively short. Water levels on the Amazon tributaries typically control the fishing accessibility, and the watershed's size, water source and topography determine the fluctuations and impact. In the upper regions of some tributaries and their lagoons, dense rainforests hem in the fishing waters.

There are some 22 major tributaries of the Amazon that are "whitewater" rivers with poor fishing, and over 45 major "blackwater"

Of the 20 largest rivers in the world, 10 are in the Amazon Basin, and all are larger than the Mississippi River system. Located on the Rio Negro is the Anavilhanas Archipelago, which is formed by about 400 islands.

tributaries throughout the Basin that offer excellent peacock bass fishing and minimal pollution. The most productive "blackwater" tributaries and lagoons get their tannin-stained colors from acids leeched from forest litter. The black waters are low in dissolved nutrients, which combined with the low acidity, makes the water very soft.

The "whitewater" rivers, which normally look brown, get their muddy color from suspended sediments carried down from the Amazon headwaters in the Andes Mountains. A few blue-water tributaries flow from the rocky south of Manaus, and they may be very clear.

The Basin waters producing the best fishing for peacocks are generally lagoons. If the lagoons have relatively clear, tannin-stained water, regardless of the color of the adjoining river, the peacock fishing should be good. In normal conditions, the larger peacock bass haunt the relatively remote lagoons, lakes and coves off the river channels during the prime dry season.

Negro, Xingu, Madeira and Other Large Tributaries

One of the largest Amazon tributaries is the Rio Madeira, which is about 2,000 miles long. Among other giant tributaries are the Negro, the Jurua, the Purus, and the Xingu. The Madeira watershed and its numerous

At low water, the sandbars and pools of the smaller tributaries make a river look very interesting from the air.

igarapes (or smaller tributaries) offer excellent fishing in the late summer and fall months.

The Rio Negro is one of the most popular fishing locations due to its proximity to Manaus, its abundant smaller igarapes, islands and lagoons and to the population of peacock bass present. Located on the Rio Negro is the Anavilhanas Archipelago, which is formed by about 400 islands. At low water, the islands reveal white sand beaches and canals that intersect the region like a mesh. Fully one-half of the islands are submerged during the river's high water period, and navigation is always a considerable challenge. In the upper region of the Negro in the Amazonas Territory of Southern Venezuela lie the Casiquiare and its great tributaries. This watershed is the home of the Yanomami Indian tribe and very big peacocks also.

Another place to experience the mysteries and wilds of the Amazon Rainforest is the 2,200-mile long Xingu River, which flows from Mato Grosso State through the South Central region of the state of Para northward. The Xingu cascades through 16 major rapids, and its largest tributary, the Iriri, is a 1,250-mile long river with 12 significant rapids. These are just a few of the good fishing tributaries of the Amazon mentioned in this text.

All of the tributaries in Brazil's Amazonia Region go through two seasons: the wet and the dry (fishing season). Most tributaries draining the states of Para, Roraima and Amazonas fluctuate substantially over the year. High water is bad news for peacock bass fishermen, so knowing the water levels on a specific tributary prior to the trip can make a big difference in enjoying a productive adventure or wisely canceling an undoubtedly unsuccessful trip. Late rains during the beginning of the dry season or "off-year" rains in the middle of the dry season can cause problems. Peacocks may scatter into the flooded jungle timber and become difficult to catch.

Unparalleled Diversity

The diversity of the Amazon River Basin is beyond belief to many. While the Basin's tropical forest covers only 7% of the earth's dry surface, it contains nearly 60% of all life forms of the planet. No other region in the world has such diversity, and only 30% of them are known by science, according to my sources.

While you view millions of trees from above, a vast ocean lies beneath much of the rain forest canopy, and that is the Amazon system. The Amazonas region, called by some "Nature's Premier Botanical Garden," has 25,000 confirmed plant species, from 200-foot-tall hardwood trees to 100-foot-high palm trees, to various grasses and the tiniest of miniature orchids. Over 25% of all pharmaceutical substances used in medicine today are extracted from the Amazon Rain Forest.

There are some 15,000 known species of fauna in the Basin. About 10% of the world's birds are found in the watershed, including large ducks (called patos in Brazil), kingfishers and others you may (or may not) recognize. Parrots, such as macaws, toucan, green papagayo and parakeets, are numerous in the skies, and water birds, such as heron and scarlet ibis, creep along the shallow shores and pristine backwaters of the lakes and lagoons in the rich biodiverse areas of the Amazon Basin.

Approximately 1,200 species of butterflies share those skies. Large beautiful Blue Morphos butterflies sporting fluorescent purple wings are common sights along the forest shore in some areas. Much of the rainforest's diversity is found high in the treetops. Several million kinds of insects dwell in the forest's upper stories, along with untold number of animal species.

Animals, Mammals & Reptiles

Although one-fourth of the world's mammals live in South America, much of the exotic wildlife, including mammals, are nocturnal and not commonly seen by visiting anglers. In the darkness, the remote parts of the Amazon jungle come alive with its nocturnal predators on the prowl. Jaguars, boa constrictors and other menacing "demons" of the night creep across the jungle floor in search of their nightly meal. Exotic animals and reptiles crawl out of their dens, holes and other daylight hiding spots.

The best tributaries have many small, d e e p - w a t e r lagoons tucked into their forest perimeter along them. Often the prime waters are in lagoons that have deep banks (during low water) and shallow, narrow cuts into them, posing restricted access.

Seldom will you spy a jaguar, sloth, ocelot, giant anaconda or other exotic night "patroller." I've seen one large jaguar, two sloths and one anaconda in all my trips throughout the Basin. The interesting sloth is a slow-moving animal that hangs upside down from branches by using its long claws. I have also seen the fairly rare anteater (with long snout), a small deer, marmoset monkeys, and a manatee. I have come across several capybara (largest rodent in the world weighing up to 100 pounds) and a few tapir (large pig-type animal with short trunk) in my ventures.

Otters, caiman and alligators (check them out at night by gazing at the dots of iridescent light on the water's surface and adjacent banks), and tribes of monkeys, including the noisy howlers, are common sightings along some of the smaller tributaries with flora-laden jungle adjacent. In the waters with peacock bass and frequently seen from the boat are freshwater stingrays, which can be dangerous to waders. Not seen nearly as often are electric eels, which are also dangerous to mess with.

Gray freshwater porpoises are frequent visitors along most rivers and open lagoon areas. Another fairly common sighting may be the most interesting, the boto porpoise. Botos are the largest of several freshwater porpoises in the Amazon, and their bodies are bright salmon pink. I did a double take when I first saw one of the creatures swimming beside my boat.

A few of the Amazon tributaries in the eastern and southern parts of Brazil have watersheds through rocky, hilly terrain. Peacocks are usually smaller, but the variety of "exotic" species is more prevalent in waters that offer islands, waterfalls, eddies, boulders and turbulence, with a minimum of quiet lagoons.

Fish Of The Amazon

There are 3,000 species of fish - about one-third of the world's total - in the Amazon Basin. Most fish in the Amazon environment have either offensive weapons such as needle-sharp teeth, poison pointed spines, or they possess superior maneuverability and/or speed. In the rainforest jungle waterways, the tough species survived and the weak are ancient history.

While the Amazon watershed offers good to excellent peacock bass in probably 80% of its tributaries and basin, the fishing operations cover perhaps 5% of the Basin. You will find a big variety of fish in the rivers and lagoons of Brazil. Besides peacocks, you may tangle with aruana (arawana), a tarpon-like fish with a "clubby" tail that grows to 25 pounds; pescada, which look like drum and grow to 20 pounds; pacu, a bluegill-like fish that runs to 20 pounds in moving waters; matrincha, a shad-like fish indigenous to Brazil that grows to 12 pounds; and corvina, a drum-type fish that grows to 10 pounds.

You also may catch several kinds of piranha, which are the embodiment of evil, both predator and scavenger. The most dangerous is the caribe or red-bellied piranha. I've been in the water with the piranha nearby, as have many visitors to the Amazon, and there is very little to worry about unless you are bleeding or "oozing" or frantically flailing. There are 35 species of piranha including the silver and black which are the two most common types caught in the Basin. A note of interest is that there are 24 towns, rivers and mountains named after this cannibal fish.

Sporty catfish are often caught on lures, including suribim, a strikingly-patterned catfish that can exceed 150 pounds, piraiba, dourada, jau, and pirarara (red-tail). Other species occasionally caught include bicuda (the fish with a bird-like beak), the golden-colored tabarana, payara (called cachorra in Brazil), jacunda, tambaqui (pronounced "tom boc key"), a fruit eater that resembles a dark, freshwater drum, morocoto, trairao (or trieda), a bowfin-type fish, and sardinata.

The pirarucu (called paiche in Peru) reportedly grow to over 10 feet long and weigh up to 800 pounds. It is one of the largest freshwater fish in the world and difficult to catch. Adult fish typically average seven feet in length and weigh over 330 pounds, and they seldom strike at lures. For centuries, Amazon natives have filed their fingernails with the fish's scales, which are very much like sandpaper. The scales' abrasive and resistant surface enables the prehistoric-looking pirarucu to survive for many years in the Amazon. There are, fortunately, also many other varieties of colorful forage fish for the peacock to feed on.

Not Just Wilderness

Tributaries pour in to the Basin from remote reaches north and south, but the Amazon Basin is not just fish, fauna and wilderness. Although South American Indians may be present in some areas, Manaus, a city of 1.2 million people, is located on the Negro River. Founded in 1669 on the site of a fort built by the Portuguese to ward off invaders, it was once the center of the Brazilian rubber (latex) trade. Manaus is hot and humid year-round and has an average temperature of 85 degrees.

The population centers of Manaus, located about 1,000 miles inland, and Belem (which has about 1-1/2 million people) offer resort hotels and, unfortunately, large commercial fish markets. The facts are that for productive angling, you have to fish at least two hours by boat away from areas worked by the commercial fishermen. That can mean a few hundred miles from Manaus. Local subsistence fishing seems to have little impact on the fishing in most tributaries.

Sportfishing in the Amazon cannot be a spontaneous pursuit. It would be difficult for people to go to Brazil to try to fish a productive area on their own without booking through a fishing operator. If they don't speak Portuguese and have access to a boat, it would be impossible. There

Some lowland areas in the Amazon have numerous land-locked lagoons at low water times (the dry season), and some operators fish such lakes or ponds. Productivity can be fantastic or nil, and it can change from one dry season to the next. Many of the isolated lagoons are beautiful.

are very few sportfishing guides in the Amazon Basin, and the best ones are contracted to the established fishing tour operations. There are no marinas or boat rental places in the interior Amazon region of Brazil.

In Manaus, there are a few tourist opportunities: The Natural Science Museum, the Teatro Amazonas Opera House completed in 1896 and rebuilt in 1929, the floating port, and the Indian Museum. The "Meeting of the Waters" of the Solimoes and Negro rivers, which form the Amazon about 10 miles east of Manaus, is an interesting and unique sight from the air. The silty, gray/brown Solimoes waters do not mix with the clear black Negro waters for many miles downstream from their merging. Finally, the rivers meld to form a massive river.

However, combine the massive territory of the Amazon Basin with a mostly third-world infrastructure that greatly impacts logistics, and you can appreciate the minimal level of explorations and development of fisheries and fishing operations. It's here on the remote tributaries of the Amazon where an angler has an excellent chance of catching 25 to 30 peacock bass per day on topwater lures, with an opportunity to land a giant (or two) ranging from 15 to 25 pounds. And that is the basis of my love of the Amazon!

Chapter 1

FLOATPLANE JUNGLE BASS ON THE CUIUNI

Giant Rainforest Peacocks Swim Near The Floating Cabin Barges!

Two tribes of howler monkeys were roaring at each other over the tree-shaking winds that had just swept into our isolated lagoon. My cast had allowed for the strong wind, but a gust pushed it another 10 feet off the drop at the edge of the sandbar island. I popped the big topwater plug twice, further disturbing any "quiet" of the black water environment that the surface-ripping winds hadn't already destroyed.

A giant fish "blew up" on the Big Game Woodchopper, launching the plug skyward and 30 feet closer to the boat and leaving behind only a huge boil marking its spontaneous appearance. I quickly reeled in the heavy line and lure and returned the wooden "irritant" to the precise spot of temptation. The big peacock bass exploded again on the plug as it moved over 6 feet of water, and it "hung on" this time.

I too hung on, as it tore up the bar along the drop and then headed shallower toward timber. The fish ran well back under two large, overhanging tree branches, but fortunately, there were no long limbs under the extended surface branches. I put a lot of pressure on the fish to keep it away from the noticeable entanglements near shore. Then my guide, Juan, moved the boat away from the potential obstructions for the remainder of the battle.

Luckily, the fish swam in and out of the top of more limbs on the deepwater side of the drop without snagging my line. I didn't realize how big it was until it started to pull drag and eventually showed itself. A few minutes later, I brought a weary 20-½ pounder up to the gunwale. Juan reached over and grabbed the huge fish. It was photo time. I rushed a few

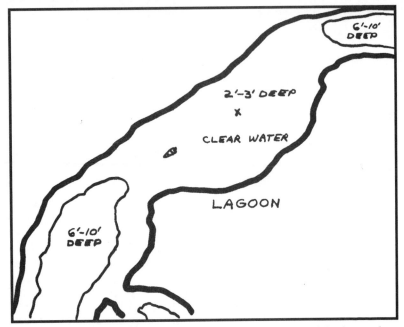

Figure 1- One very large, narrow lagoon that I fished had two deep stretches of water located two hundred yards apart. On one trolling pass from the back deep-water area, I just decided to leave my lure in the water over a shallow flat that varied from 30 to 36 inches deep. We were slowly motoring over to the other deep section of the lagoon when, about midway, an 18 ½ pound peacock came out of nowhere in the crystal clear water to smash my topwater. Lesson: Don't give up totally on topwaters in shallow water!

shots and placed the film star back into the tiny black water lagoon, just before the storm arrived.

I barely had time to don my rainsuit as the winds swept driving rain in our face. Juan motioned toward the shoreline cover, and with my nod, headed our aluminum boat into a somewhat-protected canopy of trees. We sat in the driving rain for 20 minutes, which gave me ample time to reflect on the success of the morning.

I had had quite a day on the lagoons off the Cuiuni River (also spelled Cuini or Cuiuini) in north-central Brazil. Of the 12 peacock bass that I had hooked and released, an 11 and 12 pounder were among the small specimens. I also took a 16 pounder, a 16 1/2 pounder and one of 18 ½ pounds. A trolled topwater plug fooled the latter fish. I was working it from the moving boat about 80 yards back over only three feet of water in a long, 200-yard wide lagoon. Some may have thought me crazy to be trolling a topwater in crystal clear water over a narrow flat that shallow!

Fry "Balls" & Piranha Bursts

The 16-½ pounder smashed my topwater as I popped it through a "ball" of peacock bass fry on the surface. It was like three other big peacocks I had taken earlier in the week from others balls of young. Peacock bass parents will slam anything coming near their fry post-spawn as they are in a full-protection mode. It's an interesting phenomenon to watch and to take advantage of. Newborn fry of one inch long or so and even older fingerlings up to 6 or 8 inches in length will form a "ball" and move about the surface of the lagoon with one or both parents swimming alongside or just beneath.

There may be 2,000 tiny fry in a 2-foot diameter ball moving on the surface. When winds are light, they can be readily seen. When the surface ripple is substantial, then it is very difficult to see, even by native guides with trained eyes. When danger approaches, the tiny fish will swim inside the mouth of the parent until it is safe to venture back out. If the angler can see the "ball" of fingerlings moving along the surface and toss a lure within 5 or 6 feet of it, the protective peacock parent will explode on the foreign source of anguish. An accurate caster may catch and release three or 4 of these "protective" fish a day during optimal times.

Another interesting phenomena are "piranha bursts". On several occasions on the Cuiuni, a school of 8 or 10 piranha would burst into the air, leaping above the surface three feet or so, frantically trying to escape a big peacock that is right on their tail. The feeding activity might continue as the school disperses in mid-air a couple of more times until another giant swirl from the predator ends the chase.

At active times, peacocks are just easier to catch. On this trip, I often cast to commotion in one form or another and caught big peacocks. So did several others in our group, and in fact, anglers Ted Schmidt, John Mihalic, Tonia Teke and Debbie Kemp all caught and released 20 pounders.

One interesting, non-twenty pounder blew up on my "trout" colored Big Game Woodchopper knocking it 5 feet up in the air and 15 feet closer to my boat. I yelled at my partner for that day, Ron Teke, of Silverthorne, CO, to "cast quick" to the fish, knowing my lure was probably out of its range. His topwater plug quickly landed near the settling ripples, and the fish immediately exploded on it. By then I had reeled in my loose line and lure and tossed back again to the one triggering spot. The 17-pounder again exploded on my lure, and we were hooked up solid then.

The key to such productivity in the rainforest is usually being very observant about what is going on in the aquatic environment and changing lures and presentations in typically prime areas. If I toss a topwater bait into an obvious fish-holding area several times without a strike or a follow, I'll switch off and throw a submerged bait such as a large 6-inch minnow bait or a one-ounce Pet spoon. Frequently, I'll entice a strike that way.

Thoroughly fishing an area is always wise when fish signs are apparent. During daylight hours, larger peacock bass are almost always in the deeper waters of a lagoon or slow-moving waterway. Smaller fish are tighter to the bank in shallower water around or in protective cover. I fish for the bigger ones.

Conquering The Cuiuni Lagoons

That week while fishing the lagoons off the Cuiuni River west of the Rio Negro, I personally caught over 60 peacock bass, with 25 of them weighing over 12 pounds each. Perhaps even more impressive to this frequent Amazon visitor is that 18 of those fish were larger than 15 pounds, and three peacock bass exceeded 20 pounds. It was one of my very best trips for peacock ever!

Getting there was not an easy task. It involved an overnight flight to Manaus, Brazil; then our group of 8 anglers boarded a large amphibious plane, took off from a small paved runway and landed on a twisting string of waterway deep in the Amazon Rain Forest. Guides in our fishing craft met us at the floatplane and took us to our floating camp, four large cabin tents set up on floating barges tied up to a nearby sandbar. After watching our floatplane sail off over the jungle canopy, we set up our rods and tackle and were fishing the remote waters that afternoon.

The very comfortable tent cabins were towed by a large riverboat about 20 miles upstream almost daily to relocate the "home base" to mostly-unfished waters. All are pulled up on a serene sandbar each evening and staked out to prevent their drifting away. The floating cabins with private showers, toilets and beds are equipped with a 12-volt battery to power lights, fans and shower pumps. A generator powers the battery chargers, the cooking barge and the dining tent barge.

Each afternoon, our group of anglers would sit back in lounge chairs on the sandbar and swap stories about the giant fish taken or lost that day. Laying in the comfortable bed at night, listening to the sounds of nocturnal creatures such as frogs in the jungle and the fish feeding on

Minnow-type baits are sometimes effective when peacocks are not aggressive. The author's 20-pounder was taken with a "come-back" bait thrown to a Cuiuni fish that had swirled on, but not taken, a big topwater plug.

small minnows along the shoreline beside your cabin barge is an interesting experience. Such sounds lull you to sleep. A generator far off in the forest offered a rhythmic hum.

At least once each night, a riverboat with tropical fish gatherers went chugging by with spotlight waving at the edges of the jungle as it made its way downstream. They were relocating their boat and small fishnets to search locations nearer Barcelos, the renowned "tropical fish capital of the world".

Post-Rain Maneuvers and Tactics

From our first afternoon on, the week was cast and blast. We would cast a big plug and the peacock would blast it. The fish that week were very active, despite a few intermittent rains. Often I noticed a few fish playing around off the deep drops along sandy beach points and would cast to them for a hookup. For maximum productivity, I typically cast into waters about three feet deep where the bottom disappeared from sight.

G uides in their fishing craft meet the clients at the floatplane and transfer them to the floating camp. The large float planes are very comfortable for rides in and out of the week's fishing waters.

Not all of my big fish were landed however. I distinctly remember a 17-pound plus fish and one just over 20 or so that pulled off. Then, there was another monster every bit as large as the 20's I caught that week that spit out my plug just 10 feet from the boat.

Sun seems to be everything to the peacock bass. It is what incubates the eggs on the bed, initiates the plankton food chain for the fingerlings and then increases the metabolism of the fish so that they can feed and grow. That's why a day without sunshine in the rainforest is often a poor fishing day. Peacocks sleep all night in the shallows away from large nocturnal predators that roam the deep. The sun wakes them up each morning, and if dark overcast skies meet the break of day, the peacock are slow to get started. They need the sun to fully get going, much as some humans need a shot of caffeine to become wide awake and/or be able to function intelligently.

We know that peacocks are not active at night, and, in my experience, they are usually less active under heavy cloud cover or during heavy rains, even later on in the afternoon. In hard rains, even the aggressive, "territorial" type strikes are hard to come by. One reason might be that the peacock may not hear a large topwater plug ripping through the surface waters. Small fish are usually more aggressive than big ones in a heavy rainstorm. An exception may be a brief, "refreshing" type shower that occurs during a hot afternoon and has minimal impact on the feeding activity of all sizes of peacock.

During that week on the Cuiuni, I believe that the fish were holding at the edge of the sandbars after rains and on overcast days. When the air temperatures were "cool", the fishing was correspondingly slow. After a rain, the fish appeared to want to move into the shallows to take

The floating tent cabins are towed during the day and staked out along a sand beach at night. You might call this luxury camping. All tents offer private bathrooms and showers and two beds with fans overhead.

advantage of the sun's heat in order to get their metabolism going again. As a result, they were positioned near the edges of the breaks off sandbars and points and in a fairly aggressive posture there. We were fishing at the beginning of the rainy season and the sky moisture came down on us almost every day on the Cuiuni.

Striking Reasons In Shallow Waters

There are several types of striking action that an angler may come across on the Cuiuni and in fact, on most peacock bass waters. The reflex action of a territorial strike is one where the fish just wants to destroy something in its "space" which may be a 50-yard square area in a small, deepwater lagoon. The territory also may be a "mobile" space that is everything within 40 or 50 feet of the fish, as it is moving about.

The peacock will also strike out of hunger in the interest of feeding or out of opportunity. When the latter arises, they will take advantage of a wayward baitfish or an artificial lure resembling one. This is a foraging behavior. Finally, a third type of striking reason is due to their protective post-spawn nature discussed earlier.

Submerged lures are often better for feeding-type strikes or for enticing a less than super aggressive fish, while topwater plugs may generate any of the aforementioned types of strikes. Both work on "balls of fry" if you can get the lure on the front edge of the fry or within a few feet of it. If the cast lands 10 feet away, it generally won't produce, and even if it lands on the fry ball, it may or may not be struck.

Hooks on all lures need to be extremely sharp and if they are too heavy, they do not hold a point well. It is best to replace a dull, heavy hook with one that is very sharp. In fact, I've found that many lures you may buy at the tackle store will not have sufficient hooks to hold the largest peacocks you may catch. A few may have hooks that are too heavy to keep sharp. Carrying extra replacement hooks in your tackle box is a good idea.

The 18 1/2-foot long aluminum flat bottom boats with wide casting decks are comfortable to fish from, and handle the small waters well. The 15-hp outboards and trolling motors employed offer adequate power to get around the numerous lagoons and false river channels that lace the Cuiuni. In five full days of fishing, we fished 25 lagoons and passed up another 25 that were too shallow, too small or were being fished by our fishing companions.

About 40 percent of the lagoons were too shallow, and even in the deep lagoons, about 25 percent were too shallow to hold big fish. The water was about three feet below the base of the trees in most cases, but there are many fallen trees and submerged laydowns, particularly in the deepwater lakes off the Cuiuni. The many oxbows are basically lagoons at low water with no flow through and during the high water, rainy season, they become parts of the river with current flow.

When waters are low and relatively clear at the end of the dry season, rain will increase the water level and bring in more murky waters. Both are not favorable for catching peacock bass. When the forest floods as water levels increase substantially, the fishing is over. Most fish then move back into the jungle to feed, and the angler just can't reach them.

The Mark of A Great Guide

Great guides in the rainforest usually make for a great trip. The Cuiuni River guides, like all great ones, notice subtle signs of feeding activity and "balls" of fry swimming along on the surface. They also make suggestions to the angler about casting to points, sandbars and cuts and when to repeat casts to such obvious fish-holding spots. They are wise to the tactic of casting several times to a big fish that has given its location away or to a second big fish "partner" of one that was just caught and released. Both concepts are the smart thing to do when after big peacock bass.

The excellent guides also watch any hooked fish and move the boat away from battle dangers such as large laydowns, brush piles, rocks, etc.

Ron Teke hefts a 16-pound Cuiuni River peacock that came after his big Woodchopper numerous times before getting hooking.

They are very observant about potential problem obstructions and try to alleviate any interaction with such on casts or from hooked fish by handling the boat appropriately. They will raise the trolling motor when a lively peacock is near the boat and is seemingly "hot". They are very aware of what the fish is doing during the battle and always ready with the net or BogaGrip when the peacock is off the gunwale.

The guides are observant about a knot or abrasion in your line, a bent hook or other lure problem and will even "tune" your topwater plug if it is not running right due to a slightly bent propeller. They'll add a little more cup to the blade with a pair of pliers to make the right (most productive) sound. They are very adept at suggesting lures and lure changes. Like many anglers, I carry four rods with different lures on each at all times while in the boat. That sometimes requires a lot of guide attention.

My Rio Cuiuni guide, Juan, who has worked with visiting peacock bass anglers for over six years, was very "in tune" with my thought process about which lure to toss at a specific piece of cover and when to change to another for a different spot or for another shot at the same spot. He seemed to also know why big fish were in the places we found them and what might be the best lure to entice a strike from them, or at least,

The author admires one of his three 20-pound plus fish that he caught and released from Cuiuni lagoons. He also caught 15 others between 15 and 19 1/2 pounds during the productive week.

... his thought process was identical to mine. He was knowledgeable about fishing and fishing lingo, which is refreshing and different from most of the guides I fish with in the jungle.

Prime Timing, Options and Information

There was plenty of wildlife to enjoy during our fishing days on the Cuiuni River such as monkeys in the trees, a capybara along one beach, a few iguana and two snakes. Overhead, green parrots raced everywhere; toucans, pato ducks and macaws, 9 in one large group, colored the skies. A few dolphins mostly in the river channels and a 9-foot caiman were waterscape enhancements.

The prime fishing season on the Rio Cuiuni is January through March, but the water level can play havoc with the fishing and access to it. During high water, peacocks swim far back into the forest, while extremely low water levels prevent even the small boats from covering a

Most guides are very good at finding sizable fish and operating the boats. Juan is one of several who are at this operation.

lot of water from its cabin barge camp base. An 8-day itinerary will put you on fishing water 5 1/2 days. If the waters of the Cuiuni are not conducive to great fishing, the River Plate Outfitters operation simply moves to better waters. Agent Rod & Gun Resources offers three of the fly-in cabin barge operations on various rivers throughout the Amazon, and they are generally booked from mid-August through March, according to owner and avid peacock bass angler J.W. Smith.

Last year's big fish on a Rod & Gun trip was a 26 ½ pound peacock caught on the Rio Urubaxi, which is another Rio Negro tributary that lies just north of the Cuiuni. Other rivers that Rod & Gun/River Plate Outfitters fish are the Araca, the Macucau, the Jufari, the Jatapu, the Caures, the Unini, the Jau, the Amapa, the Marmelos and the Madeirinha. That's quite a list, but with three operations going at the same time, they need several options to offer the very best fishing under existing water conditions.

To find out more about the Amazon Peacock Bass Safari, contact J.W. Smith of Rod & Gun Resources, 206 Ranch House Rd., Kerrville,

TX 78028; Phone (800) 211-4753; FAX (830) 792-6807; e-mail: venture@rodgunresources.com or visit their website at www.rodgunresources.com. To find out more on Luhr-Jensen's Big Game Woodchoppers, contact Luhr-Jensen & Sons, Inc. at 800-535-1711 or check their website at www.luhrjensen.com.

Chapter 2

RIO ARACA "BIG FISH" FLY-OUTS

Fly-Outs, A/C Lodge Comfort and Ever-Changing Action

Activity means a lot to the successful peacock bass angler. That's why I was very optimistic when my guide Careca and I entered the small lagoon off the upper Araca River to find surface feeding activity along one deep shoreline. The fish chasing the baitfish didn't appear to be gigantic, but they were "hot" on the tail of their forage. We motored quietly toward the surface commotion.

I heaved my big clown-colored surface lure in the general direction of the activity and began working it back toward our aluminum boat. Seven casts later, I was still searching for the feeding fish, spray casting from the shore near where we had seen some activity to the deep waters in the middle of the small lagoon. One good rule of thumb when fishing peacock is to go relentlessly after fish that give themselves away visibly.

On my 25th cast, this one to the middle of the lagoon in front of me, a peacock with broad shoulders rolled on the plug and dove for the deep, which was some 10 to 12 feet in that lagoon. I was thinking "low-teens" for this fish that struck relatively quietly and then moved off slowly pulling some drag. Then, it charged off and pulled drag from my reel continuously for 40 feet more.

"Big fish," Careca shouted, as I then started thinking "upper-teens" for this unseen peacock bass. It rolled far out as I regained line, but it wasn't until I had him near the boat that he jumped and exposed his full body.

"Oh yeah," I said. "It's at least 20! Use the net," I commanded.

My guide smiled and readied the net. Again, he repeated, "Big fish!"

*T*he upper Araca River is a beautiful little river with plenty of sandbars and lagoons at low water. A fly-out trip to this area from the lodge is not to be missed.

The fish swam by the 16-foot long boat five times, just out of reach of Careca's net. I turned it each time, but the peacock was very suspicious of our waiting net. Finally, it was over. My guide weighed the monster on his certified BogaGrip scales and showed me proudly the "big fish". It weighed 23 pounds and was a true giant. That peacock was my largest of the week and at the time among my three largest ever. I was happy.

Perseverance does pay off, as that experience proved. But with the water dropping about three or 4 inches each day on the Araca, it paid off on most days.

I finished that day with 15 and 16 pounders also and a big butterfly of 7 pounds in addition to some smaller ones. I had taken a plane ride with two other anglers that morning to check out the fishing near the Araca Outpost camp that Amazon Tours had set up. This Fly-Out service

Louisianan Uncus Favret shows off his 24-pound Araca monster to friend Ky Douocet. Big topwater plugs were certainly the ticket for this fish and a slightly smaller 22-pounder that he caught the same day.

offered to their clients at the Rio Araca Lodge, where I was staying, the Rio Negro Lodge and their Amazon Queen operations, worked for me that day. It was my best day for big fish during the week.

Louisianans Uncus Favret and Ky Doucet had a tough time that day on the fly-out, but don't feel sorry for Uncus, who caught and released a 22 pounder and a whopper 24 pounder on our second full day at the lodge. His 24-pound 3-bar beat out my fish for big one of the week. He also caught a 20 pounder on the following day. Only my partner, Bill Lewis, did better in terms of 20 plus pound fish, as he garnered four big beauties during the week.

Bill Lewis, on his sixth trip to the Amazon, had the "hot" hand for the week, catching the most giants, as well as the most fish of our group of six anglers. The Plano, Texas angler also caught the week's biggest butterfly, a giant 9 pounder that fought like he was a 14-pound "grande". His big butterfly came from the inside bend of a "moon-shaped" sandbar at the mouth of a shallow, tiny lagoon. All of his 20's were memorable, but the last one of the trip was the most.

Last Dance, Last Strike

We were hitting our last spot of the day about 25 minutes downriver from the lodge on the last day of our trip. Fishing had been fairly tough that day; Bill had caught 8 peacocks earlier and I had only three to my credit. None had been large.

The author caught this 23-pounder on the upper Araca on a giant clown-pattern topwater on his 25th cast to the center of a small lagoon. Perseverance paid off.

Our guide pulled the Tracker bass boat in behind a long, submerged sandbar that jutted into the Araca near the mouth of a small shallow lagoon. Two or three cuts up to 5 feet deep ran through the mostly submerged sandbar. The guide dropped the trolling motor and we moved toward the only dark water on the bar that lay in mostly two feet of water. Our first casts met with success.

Bill and I had two strikes and two small peacock. About 10 minutes later, we had hooked and landed another 9 peacock bass. Most were two to 4 pounds, and the late-day action was refreshing after such a tough day on the water. We lost at least that many after strikes, so it was non-stop. But our time was running out.

"Dos mais", the guide directed, "y vamos!"

My next cast garnered a strike and I quickly landed my fish. Bill's following few casts were slightly off the mark and found no activity.

"Guess I'll have to catch the last one, so we can go in," I goaded him. "Last cast."

With two company-owned floatplanes, Amazon Tours offers fly outs to even more remote waters for anglers that want to get away from the lodge. Most of the fly-outs are highly productive.

I twitched my plug twice, had the small blow up and my fish jumped throwing the plug back at the boat. Bill twitched his topwater plug and got a larger explosion. He set the hook and hung on as a fish far out of the cookie cutter mold of the others took off through the shallow water over the bar. Five minutes later, our guide slid the net under his big fish, and we all realized it was much bigger than any of the others on that bar. It weighed 21 pounds and was his biggest for the week and biggest ever. His last cast of the trip was truly very memorable. We left the active fish and headed on in to pack for our trip home.

Big Fish Week

All in all, we had a very productive week. Our group of six caught a total of 407 peacocks, and 8 were larger than 20 pounds – quite a feat for six anglers. I ended up with 48 peacocks in about 5 ½ days. Only 20 fish from 10 to 19 pounds were boated by our small group, which is a little low considering the large numbers of fish and of giants over 20 pounds. We did work hard for the 20's though, and I believe that perseverance helped pave the way. Bill's and my guide for most of the week was Alcindo, and he would "camp out" on a likely looking spot or one in which we had noticed some movement or activity.

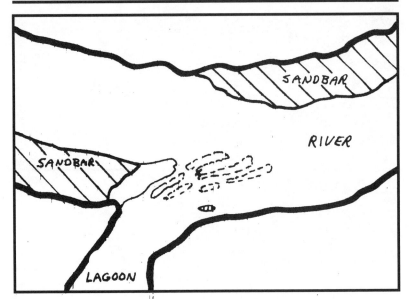

Figure 2 – This is a shallow river spot that held plenty of small, 2- to 4-pound speckled peacocks. Sandbars partially blocked an entrance into a lagoon, and several one foot-deep bars were also on the downstream edge of the partially submerged sandbar. Three-foot deep "troughs" between the shallow, submerged bars were where a huge school of "specks" were located, and almost every other cast from us resulted in a strike or hook-up. My partner's last cast (of the day and week) to the spot resulted in a 21 pounder. Lesson: Big guys have to eat too, and 2-pound speckled peacocks are perfect snack size!

Bill and I often made 100 casts to a sandbar point, for example, and we might or might not finally generate the strike from a monster. Alcindo simply would not leave a big fish until we had the water in a froth from our casts. On our best "numbers" day, Bill and I caught 32 peacock from small lagoons off the Cururduri River with my 16 pounder and his 20 pounder the prize catches. On the day of my fly out, Bill fished by himself and landed 70 peacocks on the same river with three large fish included, a 16-, 19- and 20-pounder.

The Rio Araca Lodge has six excellent Bass Tracker aluminum Pro Model 165 bass boats with 40 hp, 4-stroke outboards. In one or two of the remote, walk-in lakes, the lodge staff will drag-in and position a narrow 16-foot aluminum skiff. Guides simply carry in a paddle and the cooler

Texan Bill Lewis lands a giant 9-pound butterfly peacock, the week's largest of that species. He also caught four 20-pound 3-bars during the week on topwater plugs.

and tackle. In low water, there are maybe 20 land-locked lakes in the jungle. Most of the better catches from them have been quantities of 30 or 40 butterfly peacocks.

Araca Lodge Life

Amazon Tours personnel arrived with chainsaws and other tools, along with a small three-man crew of workers in mid-July and finished construction of the lodge in early November of 2002. All wood, except for tongue-and-groove flooring and walls were free-hand cut from the rainforest surrounding the lodge. The window casings and all furniture such as the bed posts and chairs were cut out of the forests and then milled at the woodworking shop at the Rio Negro Lodge and then transported to the Rio Araca Lodge by boat.

The Rio Araca Lodge is owned and operated by Phil Marsteller and his company Amazon Tours, which also owns and operates the Rio Negro Lodge and the Amazon Queen riverboat. The lodge accommodations are

The Araca Lodge is a comfortable facility perfectly positioned to take advantage of three distinct fishing areas. Plenty of 20-pounders swim in these waters!

5 air-conditioned rooms with two queen-size beds and private baths. A huge dining room, bar and lounge area lies at the other end of the same building. Up to 10 guests per week are flown into the lodge by floatplane from Manaus.

The lodge has been busy since its opening, catering to an 80% occupancy. The fishing on the Rio Araca has reportedly been good, and that the best one day catch was 80 peacock in a boat. The largest peacock caught in lodge waters has been 25 ½ pounds.

Outposts Postings & Furnished Tackle

The outpost camps are busy about two days each week. They have three guides and three 16-foot Grizzly boats with 25 hp outboards and electric trolling motors that they place up the Araca River about 50 miles which takes about 20 minutes to fly out to it from the Araca Lodge. Up

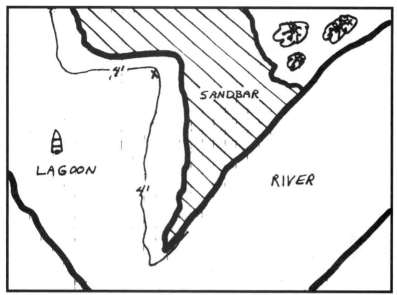

Figure 3 – Inside a medium-size lagoon off the upper Rio Araca lay a very long sandbar with a fairly slow gradient to depth. I worked the area from the 4-foot depth (which was 20 feet or so from the emergent sand) out to the boat and caught two "teeners" hanging at the 5- to 6-foot "drop" (contour line). The 16-pounder, while still in deep water, was "tucked" into the turn at a point where the sandbar projected into the lagoon 30 or 40 yards. Only little fish were playing around along the bank. Lesson: Points and pockets formed by bottom contours in relatively deep water are hangouts for giant peacocks.

to 6 anglers aboard the Queen and/or at the Rio Negro Lodge may also fly out to the outpost camp on the Araca. All tackle including rods, reels and lures are provided at the fly out locations, as well as at the lodge. Another fly out location for an outpost camp is on the upper Urubaxi River, a Rio Negro tributary that lies several miles west of the Rio Negro Lodge.

One of the unique features of all Amazon Tours operations, including the Rio Araca Lodge, is that fishing equipment is provided free of charge. The tackle available includes 6 ½ and 7 foot long heavy action rods and low-profile casting reels, plus a limited supply of spinning outfits for those that prefer such. Line on the casting reels is 80 pound test Power

Pro. They supply Woodchoppers and other Luhr-Jensen lures appropriate for peacock bass.

Just 8 months before the Rio Araca Lodge was built at the intersection of the Araca and Curuduri Rivers, two boats with four anglers flew out to the same Rio Araca area and caught 18 fish over 20 pounds in one day. That fantastic day has yet to be topped since by lodge guests.

Another operation, the Research Forest Camp, lies about two hours downstream by boat at high water, so anglers from the two fishing destinations seldom cross paths. About 50 miles north of the outpost camp lies a newly discovered waterfall off the mountain range called Serra de Araca, which has mostly flattop mountains. Discovered in January of 2001 by Phil Marsteller, who was flying the area looking for fishing spots, the waterfalls are the highest in Brazil at 870 feet. On our fly-out to the upper Araca outpost, we flew over the beautiful falls.

Clear Water Observatories

If you have all the big fish you want and want to do a neat daytrip, there is a small, crystal clear creek that enters the Araca River just 20 minutes downriver from the lodge. It takes about three hours to boat upstream through the winding creek to a beautiful, spring-fed lake. The "run" is very swift and has primarily small butterfly peacocks, along with numerous other smaller fish, such as jacunda and catfish species. The creek would be a great place to snorkel.

It's fun to watch the butterfly peacocks follow the lure and either hit it or turn away in the clear waters. You can see whether the different lures are working or not.

For more information on the Rio Araca Lodge and trip availability, contact Jim Kern at Amazon Tours Inc., 751 Canyon Dr., Suite 110, Coppell, TX 75019, phone (972) 304-1656 or (888) 235-3874, fax (972) 304-5262; or email "usa@peacockbassfishing.com".

Chapter 3

PASSING PASIMONI'S 3-BAR EXAM

Giant Peacocks Test Angler Skills In Remote Venezuelan Lagoons!

A friendly dolphin exchanging smiles with me is great at a Florida attraction or motoring from one offshore spot to another, but in freshwater, I would rather not see any smiling dolphin. South America's rivers and lagoons have numerous freshwater dolphins, and a happy dolphin is usually one that has just eaten a big peacock bass.

Two were observing my initial "shotgun" casts around the small Venezuelan lagoon that they called home. As soon as I left the Rio Paciba and entered the 150-yard wide lagoon, the dolphin frequently appeared on the surface. Frankly, I was concerned about their effect on the fishing and told my partner so. Steve Cihat and I focused our casts on the deep drops adjacent the shore of the circular lagoon anyway.

The giant topwaters chugged along on the surface making the right kind of racket – that which drives peacock bass wild. A large fish blew up on my plug and I held on to the beefy rod as it made its way toward the center of the lagoon. Jumping twice to throw the 2-ounce plug, it fought steadily in the middle of the lake where waters were between 10 and 18 feet. It pulled line twice from my cranked-down drag and headed again for the skies to toss the hardware.

Soon, I landed the peacock, quickly weighed and photographed it, and then I instructed the guide to head toward the bank. We released the fish in about two foot of water near a narrow weedbed that lay adjacent to the drop all around the lagoon. The 15-pounder was tired and moved a few feet along the shallow bottom where it stopped to rest. I felt confident that the dolphin would not make a meal of this fish. They had not shown themselves during my battle or after.

The Pasimoni and Paciba Rivers have plenty of huge boulders that are magnets to giant peacocks. These rivers off the Casiquiare (which flows between the Rio Negro and the Rio Orinoco) are the primary Amazon tributaries in Venezuela that harbor multitudes of 20-pound plus peacock bass.

Three casts later, Steve hooked another big peacock that tore line from his spool. After landing the 12-pounder, we again moved to the shallows to release the big fish. That scenario was repeated five more times over the following 90 minutes, as I landed two 12's and my partner added an 11-pounder and one that weighed 16. The dolphins did show themselves twice again, but surprisingly, never seemed to bother our fishing.

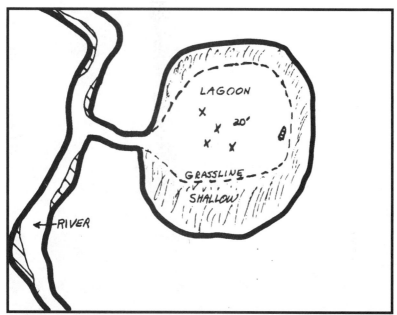

Figure 4 – "Lago Larry" is a round, deep lagoon off the Paciba River that offers giant peacocks, if you know how to catch them. It is typical of several other lagoons in the Amazonas region of Venezuela in that the giants spend the majority of their time in very deep water away from the shallows. Grassy shallows are difficult for U.S. bass anglers to pass up and throwing a giant Woodchopper over 20 foot of water may not be accepted by the same "know-it-all" anglers, but "teener" lovers like myself are wise to approach such waters by casting the surface plugs from the shallow perimeter. The big topwater will get the waters stirred up and broadcast "feeding frenzy." After catching a few on top, the wise angler will be ready to come back with submerge-type lures. Lesson: Move the boat to the shallow break and cast to the extremely deep water of a lagoon as you circle the perimeter.

We continued to move our boat slowly around the lake's perimeter casting to the middle and edges of the consistently deep water. We worked the surface of the lagoon to a "froth" with our topwaters, then switched to 6-inch long minnow baits and continued to circle and cast to the deep water. The bite slowed for about 30 minutes, and we gave thought to moving on in search of another productive lagoon...until

*D*r. Peter Kim releases a giant Paciba lagoon peacock to once again offer the fish an opportunity to provide thrills to an angler. Venezuela's Amazonas Peacocks over 20 pounds are usually longer than are their counterparts in Brazil.

something giant grabbed my hard-plastic jerkbait. It took off like a rocket straight away.

"It might be a dolphin," I said foolishly, knowing the likelihood was less than my chances in the state lottery. "Such power. Can it be a peacock? He's stripping my line!"

Dolphin Pretender's Power Drives

It was not a dolphin. I was temporarily overwhelmed by the power of the fish I had known many times over from other trips. Soon, I stopped the fish, or it just decided to turn. I gained some control then and never lost it. The big peacock didn't show itself until it neared the boat, making one jump to show off before I landed it. Steve weighed the fish at 17 pounds and measured it at 86 cm before we quickly moved to shallow water for its release.

We decided to reposition our boat more in the middle of the lagoon and cast to the drop that lay about 30 feet off the shore. Steve and I caught

Scott Swanson hefts one of his many upper "teeners" from the lagoons of the Pasimoni River. Fish in the lagoons off the river are dark and lengthy.

and released two more big peacock. And just as the fishing action had again died, we got a glimpse of one of the dolphin breaking the surface 20 yards away.

Did it have a smile on its face? I don't know because its mouth was full. It had what we thought was an 11 or 12 peacock in it! We surmised that it was one of the fish that we had caught and released. It must have swum back to deep water still very tired and ill equipped to avoid the dolphin. As the sun began to set, we headed back to our camp feeling a little sad about that.

We were fishing the Rio Paciba watershed in the extreme southern region of the Amazonas Territory of Venezuela near its border with Colombia and Brazil. Agent Scott Swanson and Venezuelan outfitter Jesus Jacotte were our host for the six fishing day Amazonas Peacock Bass Safari split between two river systems (the Paciba and Pasimoni) and two separate, sheltered camp facilities off the Rio Casiquiare. The

The author took this 39-inch long peacock from a Pasimoni River lagoon. It weighed 22 ½ pounds and was the camp's big fish of the week. It is the author's longest peacock bass that he has taken to date.

Casiquiare River is a natural connection between two of the continent's major waterways, Venezuela's Orinoco River and the Rio Negro, which flows south into Brazil feeding the Amazon River.

The Amazonas region is the home of the Yanomami Indian tribe and one of their Casiquiare villages lies on the shoreline between the Paciba and the Pasimoni. The only airstrip near the Casiquiare watershed is in the town of San Carlos de Rio Negro, and from there, anglers have to travel by boat three hours to the Pasimoni or six hours to the Paciba. The remoteness is obviously why the fishing is outstanding. There is no significant native fishing pressure on the Paciba and not even local subsistence fishing on the Pasimoni. Fortunately, the only fishing pressure is from the camp boats.

The fishing action on the Casiquiare watershed takes place in the 25 or so lagoons off the Paciba and in the 40 lagoons off the Pasimoni. The Curimoni River, which lies between the two, also offers a much smaller watershed with some giant peacocks. At the lower end of the Paciba River there is a large lagoon that is fairly productive, but the better fishing for us was in the smaller lagoons above it.

Return To The Paciba's "Lago Larry"

In the Paciba itself, there are numerous sandbars to traverse in order to move between the camp positioned at a beautiful waterfall area about two hours up river from the mouth and the prime fishing areas. When waters are low, the going is slow and guides must get out of the boat and either push or pull the craft past the sandbars. The fishing varies from lake to lake on both the Paciba and the Pasimoni. Most of the lagoons on them are within a one to two-hour run from the sheltered campsites.

You can't keep me down or away from a dynamite peacock lagoon, so after a comfortable night's sleep in our "Churuata", or open-sided, thatched-roof shelter, I headed back to my favorite Paciba lagoon the following day with another partner, Dr. Peter Kim, of Marquette, MI. We started off with our favorite Luhr-Jensen Magnum Woodchopper surface plugs, but in 30 minutes hadn't seen a swirl. I switched to a giant crankbait and pulled a 19-pounder from the middle on my first cast with it. Four casts later with a big No. 18 Pet Spoon, I hooked a 17 pounder. Peter then fooled another giant 16 ½ pound peacock with a large minnow bait and I followed that up with a 14-pounder with a similar lure.

The giant bounty was still in place. I had to ask my guide what the amazingly productive little lagoon was called. "No nombre", he replied in Spanish. He thought a few seconds more and then asked, "Como se llama?" (What is your name?) I replied, "Larry" and he said, "Este es Lago Larry!"

The guides are all Indians from the region, but all speak Spanish and very little English. Some, like mine, have a great sense of humor. The guides do a good job of positioning the boat, both for casting and trolling, and I was impressed with their knowledge of the waters and their ability to find good fishing areas. They are very good at moving the boat quickly away from any compromising entanglement when one of the giant peacocks is hooked.

Alternating Rivers & Camp Comforts

We moved to the river, where I lobbed a Tony Accetta Spoon to the edge of a shallow slough and hooked up with another giant – a 19-pounder. Then, we took off on a three-hour boat ride back through the Casiquiare to the Rio Pasimoni. In my mind, I recapped the successful morning.

The Amazonas Peacock Bass Safari camp is comfortable, but not luxurious. There is one camp with kitchen, lounge area, tables, chairs, sofas, twin beds under mosquito netting on both the Paciba and Pasimoni Rivers.

Had we stubbornly stuck to our preferred topwater plugs on that day, I believe that we would not have been as successful in such a tiny lagoon with a very limited number of giant peacocks and a couple of dolphin. Steve and I had worked the area hard the day before, but there was still some bounty left for Peter and I. Being versatile and knowing the time to alter a presentation and bait is sometimes the key to success in peacock waters!

Our rustic, but comfortable camp on the shores of the Pasimoni was very similar to that on the Paciba. Jesus built the two similar camps with splitting up the fishing time in mind. While the camps only take 8 anglers per week and the "fishing season" is only 3 months a year under normal low water conditions, the rivers and associated lagoons are small and could be over pressured. To avoid the possibility, Jesus and Scott decided that moving the group mid-week would be the conservative-minded thing to do. Fortunately, both watersheds are full of giant peacock bass, so resting one for 3 days and fishing the other caused no concern among our group of seven anglers.

The fishing on the Pasimoni was very similar in terms of our catch quantity and size of the fish during the remainder of the week. In fact, I caught my longest peacock bass ever on the final day. While Steve had taken a 21 ½-pounder from a lagoon off that river, I was still looking for a "20 plus" on this trip and decided to troll for one on the last day. Peter also wanted to increase his big fish of the week and elected to go trolling in a large, deep lagoon where we had each hooked fish in the upper teens a day earlier.

Pasimoni's Freight Train #39

About noon, the giant stopped my Red and White minnow bait dead in the water and rocketed off toward the river 800 yards away. He pulled drag from my baitcaster as though I had it set at about 10 pounds break strength. In fact, I had spooled 80-pound test Power Pro braid on my Abu-Garcia Morrum and had cranked the drag down tight. Dolphin? No, I was thinking "freight train".

This giant pulled line from my reel easier than had any other fish that week, so I had a good indication it was a worthy opponent. I finally stopped the run after a couple of minutes and then tried to regain line on an almost empty spool. Even with the premium no-stretch braid, keeping a taut line on a giant fish 100 yards away proved difficult. So did keeping the fish from heading toward fallen timber near the shore. Someone above was looking over me, because the big fish turned right before swimming into some emergent brush, as I reeled frantically to regain, make that "gain" control.

The giant did momentarily get into some brush a minute later, and my heart sank, until it swam free. The last 20 yards, I had some control. Peter helped me land the fish, weigh and measure it, and watch it swim off in good shape. The dark fish weighed 22 ½ pounds, which is very respectable, but it measured a whopping 39 inches long! While I've caught 17 peacock bass over 20 pounds, including three others weighing more on my numerous trips to South America, I had never caught such a lengthy peacock bass. Much of my peacock fishing has been in Brazil where the fish at that weight are shorter and slightly stockier, typically "only" 35 to 37 inches.

I was a happy man, and I became happier when my partner, Peter, caught a 19-pounder in the same lagoon after a quick lunch break, just an hour later. Peter had taken a few 20's on a previous trip to the same water, but this was his largest of the week. Others in our group that week caught big fish of from 17 to 18 pounds. Overall, according to our record-keeper Scott, the 7 of us caught 71 peacock over 10 pounds. I was

If you can be on the Pasimoni during the prime low water season January through March, giant peacock bass are the norm. This area is the country's best bet for giants over 20 pounds.

fortunate enough to catch 8 fish over 15 pounds which makes for a great trip and one of my most memorable for sure.

Timing The Water Levels & Weather

We caught a few more fish from the Paciba than from the Pasimoni, because the water level was lower on the former. In fact, the Paciba was a couple of feet below what many would consider "prime". It lay about 3 feet below the major tree root base in most areas, and about 75 percent of the lagoons and oxbow lakes were extremely shallow with little available depth over 3 feet. Such areas hold peacock bass but generally not the giants. As we slowly motored in the river between deeper lagoons, our prop would hit sand bottom several times. While the water was dropping in the Pasimoni, the water level seemed perfect to me. About 80 percent of its lagoons had waters deeper than 4 feet.

The weather in general was hot and sunny, but early mornings that week were sometimes overcast. Bathing in the black tannin-stained waters each afternoon was a refreshing way to cool off while under the intense equatorial sun. The rivers, particularly the Pasimoni, were surprisingly cool. I guessed it at about 78 degrees, which is cool for this long ago transplanted Floridian.

The prime "low-water" fishing season on the two rivers is January through March, but the water level can play havoc with angler success. Water levels can vary six or eight feet in just a few days on these watersheds, and high water "blows away" the fishing. During high water, peacocks swim far back into the forest while extremely low water prevents the small boats from covering a lot of water. An 8-day itinerary will put you on these fishing water 5 1/2 days. If the waters on the Paciba are not conducive to great fishing, the waters on the Pasimoni might be at a better level.

Wildlife views are many. Toucans, macaws, green parrots and other birdlife fly the skies over both rivers and there are plenty of alligators on both watersheds. Monkeys and capybara are occasionally seen along the banks. The bugs are not too bad on the rivers, but visiting anglers do need good insect lotion at dawn and dusk to keep chiggers and "no see-ums" away. Long-sleeved shirts and long pants are advisable for protection from afternoon sun and the biting bugs.

Luxury Memories & Length Boat Time

Though lacking some luxuries offered by other peacock bass operations in other parts of South America, we certainly weren't roughing it at Jesus' Amazonas Peacock Bass Safari camp. A generator-powered refrigerator and cooking stove offer safe storage and cooking functions in a separate kitchen. Tables and chairs are set up at the main shelter, which has concrete flooring and a lounge area with sofas and soft chairs. The sleeping shelter has concrete flooring, and the twin size beds are protected under mosquito netting. The jungle can be warm and humid, but it cools down nicely at night. A flush-toilet bathroom with lights adds to the comfort of both the Paciba and Pasimoni "campsites".

The travel logistics to the camps are not easy, but the time spent is well worth it. There are several non-stop flights to Caracas from Miami, and from there, after an overnight at a local hotel, guests take a four hour charter flight over the Llanos grasslands and vast Amazonas region to San Carlos de Rio Negro. There, the traveling anglers will meet up with the Amazonas Safari crew, make a quick stop at the National Guard headquarters and then embark on the long boat trip up the Rio Negro and Casiquiare to the Pasimoni or Paciba river camps.

Not all lagoons off these two productive rivers have dolphins. A few do and they are usually well fed. Fortunately, the Southern Venezuela peacocks are well fed too. They put up a battle that few anglers could forget. Such memories make for the smiles that I have!

To find out more about the Amazonas Peacock Bass Safari peacock bass fishing opportunities on the Pasimoni or Paciba Rivers, contact Scott Swanson at FishQuest!, 3375-B Hwy 76 West, Hiawassee, GA 30546; Phone (888) 891-3474; e-mail: questhook@aol.com or visit their websites at www.fishquest.com and www.peacock-bass.com.

Chapter 4

TEENERS GALORE ON THE UPPER UNINI

Giant Peacock Bass "Teams" Race For Your Topwater Plug!

My cast was like the previous 200 — medium distance to a spot some 20 to 30 feet off the closest sandbar bank. And like many before that morning in Lago Piraracu, I expected the big strike. Earlier, a 15-pounder, and soon after a 16-pounder, had jumped on the same Parrot-colored Big Game Woodchopper. My partner for the day had enticed a 13- and a 15-pounder also in the prime 9 am to 10 am "big fish" time slot. The big fish were wide awake and active. And I knew that.

The topwater splashed down and I started my rhythmic-cadence retrieve. I was able to impart only one jerk when the green-hued bait disappeared in a huge explosion. I set the hook and held on while the "obviously giant" fish tore off away from the boat. Then, it stopped. I heaved back on my medium-heavy action rod to turn the fish, but it wouldn't move.

This battle and our guide, Isaque, yelling "grande, grande, grande" from his position at the stern of the aluminum boat now had the attention of my fishing buddy Don Cutter.

"What do you have?, my partner questioned me.

"I'm not sure," I answered, as the fish again took off in another direction. "I keep trying to turn him and can't, but then, he stops momentarily. It's a really big fish, but it's fighting funny."

"I think it might be a catfish," I continued, as the fish again seemed to pause and then change course. "It's not jumping either. I stopped its run, but I just can't turn it or pull it toward me."

Finally some 40 feet out, the fish boiled at the surface, or more appropriately described, wallowed, and we noticed the broad side of a

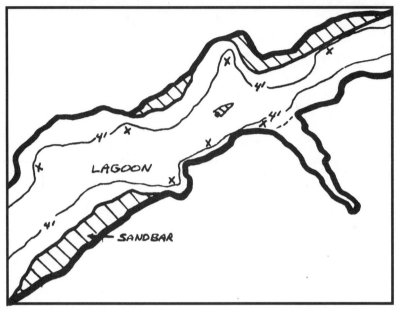

Figure 5 – Any lagoon with deep water along an irregular shoreline and numerous sandbars with good depth adjacent will be a very productive fishing spot. Fish the points, pockets and beach areas that have the deepest water nearby. When you find big fish, stick with them and repeat your coverage. In black-clear waters, "teeners" want a minimum of 4 foot of depth to feel comfortable. Large areas of deep water will allow the giants to concentrate there. Lesson: Big lagoon fish will often be found on the points and pockets near sandbars with adjacent deep water.

huge 3-bar peacock. I felt better about what I was battling, but was still puzzled by the fight.

Twenty feet off the gunwale, I was able to again bring the fish to the surface, and in the black-clear lagoon waters, the whole situation became clear. My bewilderment vanished when I noticed a second big peacock hanging onto the Woodchopper.

The "teammates" on opposite ends of the plug had obviously slammed it at the same time. I was fortunate enough to bring them to the boat without one getting off. When the two fish were aligned together and powering away from me in the same direction, I just couldn't stop them. Then, one of the peacocks would turn and stop their forward drive and

Larry's largest personal "double" on one plug is this duo. The one on the front hook weighed 13 pounds, while the one on the parrot-colored Woodchopper's rear treble weighed 17 pounds. The 30-pound catch was a unique battle and a net-full!

momentum, but even though I put all the pressure I could muster through my strong rods, I had trouble moving the twosome in my direction.

30 pounds On One Cast/One Plug

Isaque netted the two giant peacocks, as Don videotaped the action with his Sony. We then put two BogaGrips to use and I held up each peacock still attached to the plug. The largest "teammate" weighed 17 pounds while the smaller still pulled the scales down to 13 pounds. The 30 pound "double-on-one-plug" was my largest to date. In fact, I can't remember ever landing one "teener" peacock in my 12 or 15 "doubles-on-one-plug" that I have caught over the years.

Don Cutter and guide Isaque release an 18-pound Unini peacock. Most of our numerous "teeners" were taken from the many black water lagoons off the river near the houseboat base.

That experience was memorable, but so was the rest of the day, much of which was spent in that same lagoon off the Preto River about 30 minutes above its intersection with the Rio Unini. I landed another 17 ½ pounder a little later and Don captured a 16 pound giant, all on topwater fare. There was still plenty of surface activity going on while we were present, and the day's results were impressive: I had 15 peacock including 8 fish over 13 pounds and 3 others in the 10 to 13-pound category. Don, a peacock bass trip-booking agent, amassed 13 peacocks that day which included four "teeners" and the largest fish of the day, an 18-pounder.

The half-mile long Lago Piraracu is interesting from another aspect. It has a resident population of monkeys. We watched between 25 and 30 of them swinging through the trees as we fished through the middle section of the lagoon. Three huge trees along the eastern bank seemed to provide the best "hangout" for the large tribe of "macaco", as they are called in Brazil. Parrots, such as macaw, toucan and papagaios (green parrots), flew overhead in the lagoon as well as along the rivers and other lakes throughout that area. We noticed a few caiman along the banks, patos (ducks) in the skies, and freshwater dolphin in the deeper river sections adjacent the mouths of lagoons, and both tapir and capybara were also spotted along the Unini by others in our group.

The week's largest fish, this 20-pounder, was caught by "Grande" Greg Thompson, but on his previous trip, he proudly enticed a 26-pound peacock from the same waters.

The water level in the river and lagoons was excellent, but daily rains starting three days before our arrival and ending two days into our fishing did cause the river to rise about 6 inches. Some waters did get a little turbid, but the prime black-clear waters with a visibility of 18 inches or so remained in many areas.

Frazer Letzig caught his two largest peacocks ever, a pair of 18-pounders. Both struck Magnum Woodchoppers!

Chopper Classes

We tossed 7-inch long topwater Woodchoppers at points, sandbars, pockets, large laydowns, creeks and down the middle. We also threw them at any fish that we sighted. Sometimes, they would be chasing bait near one shoreline or in the middle of the lagoon, and at others, the big fish would be near a ball of fry on the surface. As usual, I would loft my cast toward any disturbed water, and often, that would result in a strike.

The Big Game Woodchoppers worked well for me all week and the parrot color seemed to be the top producer. I caught 25 teeners (peacock 13 pounds or larger), and the big topwater plug fooled all but an 18-pound, spoon-caught fish. Twelve of those fish were over 15 pounds, which makes for a very exciting week. In all, our 4-man group caught 95 peacocks over 10 pounds including 40 "teeners". The largest was taken on Day 4 when my partner Greg Thompson tossed his chopper to the edge of a small, murky-water lagoon off the upper Unini. The 20 pounder struck his bait as I set the hook into a 9-pounder a couple yards away.

The author fooled this 18-pounder with a #18 Tony Acceta Pet Spoon. Sometimes, the giant peacocks want an enticing spoon slow-rolled about 3 feet deep.

Most of our fish were taken from deep, blackwater lagoons, and the Preto seemed to offer better water quality, as the river was rising after the showers. One of the better lagoons, however, was on the Unini above the houseboat about 30 minutes by fishing boat. Greg and I helped our guide pull and push our aluminum boat sans outboard into a small lagoon alive with active fish.

Can't Keep Out Lunker Hunters

We stopped at the "almost-landlocked" lagoon on a large sandbar that blocked the entrance, and we walked to the lake's edge some 20 yards off the Unini. Seeing peacocks chasing forage in front of us, we each made a long cast to the melee. We each had an explosion, and my fish stayed hooked up, as I battled it from the sandy spit. Fortunately, I was able to turn the 16 ½ pounder and work it into shallow water fairly quickly. There, it tore up the shallows, running drag for several yards, to again be pulled back into waters just a couple feet deep.

I landed the fish, weighed it and released it back into the small lake, as other fish continued to frolic throughout. We quickly decided that extra effort to get our boat through a small 3-inch deep channel would be well worth the trouble. We quickly removed the motor, gas tanks, battery, seats, tackle bag, and cooler, and it was still very heavy. After about 10 minutes though, we had the boat in the lagoon and battery and cooler back aboard. We were ready to continue our "exploration" of those waters.

Within the following hour, fishing from the boat, Greg caught two 15-pounders and a 16-pound peacock and I caught a 14-, 15- and 16-pounder! By 10:30 am we were ready to move on. I finished that day with 13 peacock of which 8 fish were over 10 pounds. Greg, however, had an even better average weight. His 6 fish weighed 85 pounds, which calculates to an average fish of over 14 pounds each!

Who's Counting Or Even Catching Pequenos

In terms of numbers (and I only fish for "numbers" above 13 pounds), my third day of that February trip was the best with 22 peacock, but a sole 13 pounder was my only teener. On his third peacock bass trip, W. Frazer Letzig, my partner for the day was able to land two 18-pounders which eclipsed his previous personal big fish record by 4 pounds. His fish came on the "clown" pattern and peacock bass pattern Woodchoppers. His first 18 pounder was part of a double, and again I got the short end of the deal. I had cast out to a likely looking point when a 7-pounder hit my topwater.

"Throw in behind my fish quickly," I advised. He did. The second fish exploded on his topwater, and the rest is, shall we say, history. I was happy for him catching such a pretty fish and one that would establish a new record for him.

Our 4-man group caught 237 fish over the six days on the Unini, but Greg's big fish was far from his biggest. He had taken a 26 pounder in the same waters on a trip to Don Cutter's operation in November. Don and I had an excellent final day when we ran two hours up the Rio Preto and caught 28 peacocks from two small lagoons. He caught and released two 14-pounders and a 17-pounder, while I landed a 13 pounder, three 14's and an 18-pounder. The later was fooled by a #18 Tony Acceta Pet Spoon.

I watched one of the 14's follow my Woodchopper to the boat staying about 2-feet below the surface at all times. When it came time to lift the plug from the surface, I immediately started to swish it one direction and back the other. It changed directions only once before the big fish exploded on it. I had 3-feet of line off my rod tip and quite a "close-in" battle. It pulled drag but never got more than 15 feet away from the boat. I used my rod tip to dampen the powerful surges that the fish made and soon had it to the guide who employed the BogaGrip to capture the fish.

Productive Preto and Unini Rivers

The backs of the deeper lagoons were productive areas throughout the week, and I did get to fish with operation owner Frederico Bais one day on a lake one hour upriver off the Preto. I caught several teeners including a 17-½ pounder that Frazer, in a follow boat, filmed with his

*B*razilian Frederico Bais weighs a 17-pound peacock that exploded on a parrot-colored Woodchopper. Bais operates the Unini River Fishing Adventure.

video camera. I luckily "called out" the fish before casting to a prime-looking spot off an irregular point at the back of the lake. Frederico caught several big fish from that and a connected lake that yielded 3 more teeners for me.

Rio Unini and Rio Preto sandbars with adjacent deep water at the entrance to lagoons and those in the backs of lagoons held big fish during the week, and as usual, most of my big peacock that weren't chasing forage, were taken at least 30 or 40 feet off the shoreline. The Rio Unini, a tributary of the Rio Negro located some 210 miles northeast of Manaus, is roughly 200 miles long.

There are about 250 connecting lakes and lagoons throughout its course, and a waterfall and three sets of rapids lie on the lower portion, which prohibits large riverboat access to the majority of the river during all but high-water, non-fishing times. As a result, guests of the Unini River Fishing Adventure fly via charter plane to a landing strip beside the operation base, a large aluminum houseboat that is moored against the riverbank. The houseboat is located about 165 miles from where the blackwater Unini empties into the Rio Negro. There is little evidence of any villages or river residents around the areas being fished.

Houseboat Operation & Organization

The Unini River Fishing Adventure, landing strip and houseboat are owned by Brazilian C. Frederico Bais, and with exclusive agent Don Cutter's input, it has become a very efficient peacock bass operation. The modern houseboat doesn't move at all. In fact, it doesn't even have a motor. The comfortable accommodations include five spacious, two-bunk staterooms, each with air conditioning and private bathroom. There is a large dining room and lounging area, all on the same level.

Agent Don Cutter is very much a detail person when planning your trip. His Pre-Trip package includes my book, "Peacock Bass Addiction", to provide "the inside scoop on what you need to know about peacock bass fishing", several brochures on the camp, planning suggestions, a Portuguese/English translation sheet and other necessary information. He includes several luggage tags with your name and cabin number on each so that their staff will not have problems putting things in the proper place throughout the trip. Tackle bags are tagged so that they can be placed in the proper boats each morning and taken to the right room after the fishing day if you so desire.

Organization goes beyond that. Rod holders at the rear of the houseboat are marked with room numbers so that you can always find your own equipment. Guides are rotated so that each guest fishes with all guides during the week. Tony Pooran is the very efficient bi-lingual operations host aboard, and during hotel and airport transfers. There is a 24-hour radiophone connection with Manaus and a Globalstar satellite telephone system at the camp during all PeacockBassTrips.com weeks.

Fishing on the river is excellent for big catfish, if you are so inclined, and the suribim and redtail even bite during the day. Others species are also caught, and one angler even landed a 240-pound Pirarucu in late 2002. Piranhas are also very catchable.

Fishing during the week is fairly standard in that you are fishing by 10 am on the first "fly-in" day and you fly back to Manaus on the afternoon before your international flight back home. To find out more about the Unini River Fishing Adventure, contact Don Cutter at Don Cutter's Peacock Bass Trips.com, 1169 Taborlake Dr., Lexington, KY 40502; Phone (888) 626-2966; e-mail: PeacockBassTrips@bellsouth.net or visit their website at www.PeacockBassTrips.com.

Chapter 5

BLACK WATER CHALLENGE ON THE XERIUINI

Fiery Peacock Bass Action Surrounds The Macaroca and Pacao Lodges!

"Let's troll out of this lagoon and head back to camp," my friend and fishing operation outfitter Wellington Melo suggested. Our day's tally was significant. We had caught and released 30 peacock bass that probably averaged 9 pounds each. I had taken a 13 pounder off a point at the previous lagoon to top our catch, and with the "teener" that day, I was very content to motor back to the lodge before dark.

"We are going to troll out and leave," I yelled at Ed Burckle and his partner in our companion boat plugging the depths nearby. Our guide cranked the 15 hp outboard and our friends in the other boat readied their gear for the ride back, as Wellington and I loft our casts back to some deep water near the edge of the narrow lagoon. The guide pulled the lever to put the outboard in forward gear and we started our troll.

Two seconds and one twitch of Wellington's Magnum Woodchopper plug was all it took. A 12-pounder exploded on the plug almost in front of the other boat. The big fish jumped twice trying to throw its unwanted hardware, as I quickly worked my lure into the boat. Knowing that big fish often hangout in pairs, I lobbed another cast to the general vicinity of the strike in front of our companion's boat. Two twitches later, I had my reward as a monster peacock exploded on my 8-inch long custom-made Woodchopper.

Both fish cavorted around the long, 50-foot wide lagoon on the surface, as Wellington and I laughed at our fortune. We worked both fish to the boat at the same time, landing his first and then mine. Quick measurements revealed that my 32-inch long peacock weighed 14 ½

The author has found numerous hungry "teeners" on the Xeriuini River lagoons. Most favor giant topwater plugs.

pounds and had a 19 1/2-inch girth. We took a few pictures of both fish, relieved the wood plugs from their jaws and released them to fight again. It was a fitting culmination of the day.

Wellington and I chuckled about having the "atocques" or strikes right in front of Burckle's boat, but he and his partner actually had fared better than us earlier that day. Traveling with the companion boat for safety reasons, we had worked some 30 minutes pushing and pulling our craft through an overgrown, shallow creek channel that morning to

Ed Burckle caught this 16-pounder adjacent a big sandbar island in a deep-water lagoon off the upper Xeriuini River. The deep-water side of the sandbar held two giant peacocks.

access Lago Piraracu. Both guides used machetes to whack away the encroaching jungle, and teamed up to lift our boat over obstacles after we had stepped out on the bank a time or two. We even had to take both motors and the boat seats off to float the boat beneath a huge fallen tree.

Our companions entered the beautiful lagoon first, and just inside the mouth, immediately tossed their large topwaters near a sandbar with deep-water drop-off on either side. Both men got strikes, and after a good battle, Ed, from Palm Beach Gardens, FL, landed his, a 16 pounder. His partner's fish was even larger, but it threw the plug and escaped. About 200 yards further into the blackwater lake and 30 minutes later, Ed's partner landed a 13-pounder. He caught it on a point opposite of where I too landed a 13 pounder a couple of minutes earlier. Lago Piraracu was

Wellington Melo operates the Macaroca Lodge and the Pacao Lodge, both on the Xeriuini River. The Brazilian is also an avid angler, as proven by this upper "teener" catch from one of the isolated lagoons off the river.

indeed a very productive lake. Wellington and I caught and released several others in the 10 to 12 ½ pound class before we had to venture out through the creek and fish some waters closer to the lodge.

Lunch Time Is Time For Schoolers

Even lunch was hectic. We had pulled the two boats under a shade tree at the abandoned ghost village of Santa Maria to eat. The Indian village was relocated several years earlier to the Rio Branco, a larger river closer to civilization. As we took bites from our ham and cheese sandwiches, the black water river in front of us blew up with speckled peacock schoolers chasing baitfish. Burckle and I were first to grab our rods and place casts into the melee. We were rewarded with strikes of nine-pound battlers.

Twenty minutes later, the majority of my sandwich remained untouched. I had caught and released 7 of the schooling fish, and Burckle had done about the same. Our partners preferred to eat their lunches and missed out on most of the action. I finally just had to put my rod down and finish eating. As if they knew we were ignoring them, the fish also moved off to a nearby sandbar. After a short break, we did catch a few more smaller butterfly peacocks in the area before moving on. Our fishing technique that day was mostly casting, but I did get to troll some of the giant topwater plugs for some big fish on the following day.

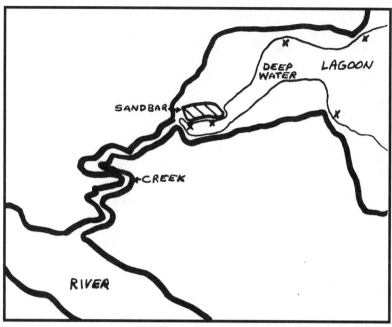

Figure 6 - The first thing to do when entering a lagoon is to check it out for deep water. Often, a sandbar or shallow sandy area will be just inside the entrance. Any quick drop in depth will provide targets for "teeners." The deep water adjacent a sandbar and/or point may be easy to locate, but other bottom contour changes along a relatively straight shoreline as this lagoon on the upper Xeriuini shows, may not. Lesson: Always fish the entrance of the lagoon and focus on deep waters, particularly if they are adjacent to a sandbar.

Good Water And Wet Skies

Cmt. Mauro Rossi, a former Brazilian helicopter pilot, and I were trolling in a lake called "Agua Boa" or Good Water. We had taken one mid-size fish when ominous clouds began moving over the dense forest canopy toward us. A heavy rain soon appeared on the horizon a mile or so away, so I started to dig out my rain suit.

A fish blasted my big topwater lure missing it. I kept twitching it. It came back after I had worked the plug 15 feet closer to the boat and exploded on the Woodchopper again. Again, it missed. Three twitches later was not a charm when again the giant knocked the plug skyward but didn't meet the hardware. Finally on its fourth try, the fish hit its target

The author helped to design the Peacock Bass pattern coloration for the Magnum Woodchopper. His upper "teen" proof of its productivity is shown.

and almost jerked my rod from my hands. I battled the leaping fish to the boat and Rossi grabbed it with my BogaGrip. He held it up and announced the weight as 14 pounds, just as the rain moved in. Wanting a few pictures, I requested that the guide hold the fish on the grip in the water while we waited for the shower to pass and some dry times for my camera.

I decided, however, to make another cast toward any of the fish's errant partners as the showers increased and the wind swept heavier rain our way. An aruana, a long, skinny fish with a fin that starts near its dorsal and sweeps around its tail and half way back along its underside, pounced on the offering. The fish is really an acrobat, out leaping about anything that swims. This five pounder did its aerial thing as the rain beat down on us and I soon brought it to the boat. Rossi landed this one with his BogaGrip. Again, I needed a photo.

Now picture this, our unfortunate guide holding two fish in the water as the rain became "monsoonal". We were out of BogaGrips, so I lay my rod to the side. Then, Rossi and I sat for 20 minutes with heads down as the rain beat down on us and filled the bottom of our small boat with 3 inches of water. I finally got my pictures when the showers waned, and the fish were released with plenty of energy to swim off. The rain reappeared later and in fact, was present during most days of our trip. We

Most of the forest lagoons off the river yield giant peacock bass. A flight in an ultralight floatplane reveals great-looking waters all along the river.

were fishing in the "dry" season, but they do call the region the Amazon "Rain Forest" for a reason.

Roraima State's Isolated Waters

The peacock-laden lagoons are located off the Xeriuini (pronounced "Sher-e-ou-ni") River in the southwestern part of the Brazilian state of Roraima. The Xeriuini flows southward into the Rio Branco just north of its confluence with the Rio Negro, one of the Amazon River's largest tributaries. The remote fishing area on the Amazon frontier is located in a protected city and federal ecological reserve. The 1,700,000 acre Xeriuini Reserve covers the 130-mile long Xeriuini River, the 90 lakes, blackwater lagoons, false channels and igarapes (creeks) within a couple hours of the lower Macaroca Lodge and the upper Pacao Lodge, along with four other rivers (Agua Boa, Catrimani, Jufari and Univini) in Roraima.

The Xeriuini is off-limits to commercial fishermen. In fact, from the small landing strip carved into the rainforest at the Indian village of Terra Preta (or Black Ground), there is no evidence upstream of any residents. You won't see other boat traffic, not even dugouts in this protected preserve.

Beyond the abandoned village of Santa Maria lies Pacao Lodge on the upstream portion of the Xeriuini River. There are five big lakes upstream of Pacao and about 8 below that fisherman there can access. Additionally there are two landlocked lakes above the Pacao Lodge and four just below that anglers can fish.

On this trip, the waters were low below the lush vegetation that surrounds each, and in fact, about 20 percent of the lagoons were probably too shallow for the giant fish that I'm usually looking for. On a previous trip one year earlier, the water was about 5 feet higher, and the water in most lagoons was far into the jungle, allowing many of the fish to be inaccessible.

Teeners, Numbers And A Monster Or Two

Our group of 7 anglers fared well on this trip to Macaroca Lodge, also called the Xeriuini Lodge. We caught and released 20 peacocks over 13 pounds including three in the 18-pound category. Burckle caught four teeners and the rest of us caught 3 with one exception. I caught around 55 peacock, and others in our group averaged about the same. A few got into butterflies schooling, catching 40 to 50 (per boat) on a couple of different days.

My partner and I had doubles on several instances, and a couple of our group reported doubles on the same plug, which is not unusual when fishing schooling peacock bass. A couple of our boats walked into land-locked lakes on the last two days and found great fishing. They helped their guide pull the boats into the lakes about 15 to 30 minutes from the riverbank. They discovered one lake was full of butterflies that would hit every cast and another had more than its share of 9 to 12 pound peacocks in its non-stop action offering.

Trophy-class fish over 15 pounds are not unusual on the Xeriuini, but even bigger fish do exist in the area. Wellington notes that he has seen peacock bass weighing 14 kilos, or 29 ¾ pounds, speared by local Indians. In fact, he decided to start his peacock bass operation on the Xeriuini when he saw one that size in the village of Terra Preta. A few of his clientele have taken 20 pounders from area lakes.

*T*he Macaroca Lodge is a comfortable facility with air-conditioned duplex cabanas for up to a total of 8 anglers per week. The lodge books trips from November through February.

Variety of Catches and Sightings

Variety also kept most of our group guessing. Speckled, three-bar and butterfly peacock bass were predominant, but an occasional piranha, trieda, bicuda, aruana, or paiche cachorra were caught and released. A couple of payara or "Dracula fish", a suribim catfish, a matrincha and a small jacunda were also taken. One angler caught a small "jacare" or caiman that finally let go of his mangled plug.

There are plenty of "botos" or freshwater dolphin and playful otters in the river and lagoons to view, and a few manatees can be seen on occasion. On one afternoon, I entered a lake to find 8 otters cavorting near the entrance. Five adults and three smaller "pups" swam along the brushy shore popping up several times to eyeball and bark at me. We also saw several jacare or alligator including some giants that appeared to be 12 or 13 feet long, a few capybara, and colorful birds patrolled the skies above the jungle canopy.

Clusters of curved palms often provided the background for the noisy parrots that raced by overhead. The numerous scarlet macaws are among the largest of South American parrots at three-foot long. Toucans, green parrots, parakeets, king fishers, heron and huge black ducks with large white under-wing patches, were also common sights. You can easily get swept away in the "nature" ambiance, until a giant peacock bass blasts your surface plug.

Comfortable, Classy Lodging

The Macaroca Lodge and the Pacao ("deep hole") Lodgeare the only two areas with structure of any kind. The Macaroca Lodge is located on Lago Macaroca and on the Igarape Macaroca (creek). The Pacao Lodge is located on the river's only 90-degree bend about four hours upstream by small fishing boat from the Macaroca Lodge.

Each lodge, to keep things quaint, accommodates only up to 8 anglers each week during the "low-water" season. Macaroca, strategically positioned in deeper downstream waters, books anglers from November through February while the Pacao books anglers from the end of September through January when waters there are ideal for peacock bass fishing.

Both first class lodges on the Xeriuini River are built right into the rainforest. The one-year old lodges offer air-conditioned duplex cabanas with private hot-water showers, comfortable beds and plenty of room to spread out. The cabanas and a restaurant/lounge/dining room are located along a hand-carved wood catwalk. A large, floating tackle storage and rigging hut is at the foot of the steps on the water. Anglers board the four shallow-draft aluminum boats at each lodge on each day. The lightweight craft are 16 and 18 feet long with 15 hp outboards, ideal for accessing some of the difficult to get to lagoons at the end of shallow, timber-strewn creeks. In the fishing boats are large coolers with iced drinks and lunch.

Wellington is a pilot who flies his two-place ultralight amphibian aircraft for reconnaissance. In fact, he and I did just that on my recent trip. We flew over some 30 lakes and other fishing locations like the "furos" or backwater river channels, checking them all out for depth and fish. We noticed several huge peacock moving through the shallows in some water bodies. We also noted numerous otters, manatees, porpoise, caiman, and catfish from the elevated viewpoint.

For more information on the Amazon Peacock Bass Fishing Adventure trip and the two Xeriuini River lodges, contact U.S. booking agent Lewis Cunningham through his website at www.reelitup.com, by email at reelitup@hotmail.com, by phone at 866-801-3209, or by writing to him at Reel It Up, 2921 Christopher Ct., Birmingham, AL 35243. Exploring the primitive and harsh Amazonas Territory in the northern Brazilian state of Roraima for huge peacock bass is an experience one cannot easily forget. That's why I'll be going back!

Chapter 6

SWEET SPOTS ON THE RIO NEGRO

First class accommodations and giant peacock bass action!

"This is a sweet spot," Phil Jensen claimed, as he landed his second peacock bass from a large, flooded-forest point. I had taken a ten pounder on my first cast to one of the openings between the inundated trees. Then, after an uneventful toss to the same area, two successive casts had resulted in two smaller peacocks for me.

My partner and I both lobbed our topwater plugs again toward the productive area. They splashed down eight feet apart, and we began our jerk and pause cadence in unison. A peacock exploded on Jensen's small Amazon Ripper plug, knocking it into the air. That fish did not come back, but we continued casting to the "sweet spot" and around the area that spread over 30 feet.

We experienced a lull of only five minutes before a big fish "blew up" on my Magnum Woodchopper. I held onto the bouncing rod as the giant bulled its way back into the flooded trees. I felt the line being raked along submerged trees as my drag groaned. I prayed.

The braid held and steady pressure turned the fish, which then took to the air behind the nearest tree along the point. I prayed again. The giant peacock bass dove into the entanglements below and again charged away from my constant pressure. After the second of three more jumps, we noticed that the big peacock was not hooked in the mouth but in the lower belly. Realizing that, I prayed some more.

Carefully, I worked the fish free of its brushy surroundings and into my guide's net. We quickly took a few pictures, weighed the 14 pounder and released it. With the evidence of fish that size on the productive

The author caught this 20 pounder just before an approaching rainstorm. His "chug and pause" retrieve called the monster from a few yards off a canopied shoreline.

point, we renewed our enthusiasm for casting the topwaters at the "sweet spot".

Two casts later, at exactly the same five foot by five foot spot, another giant exploded on my big plug. It also charged back into the trees burying itself in the heavy brush of the flooded forest. I could feel the line scraping the limbs and tree trunks as the peacock tried to rid itself of the plug and resistance.

Slowly I managed to work the fish free of its brushy habitat. From then on the fish was mine with careful attention to the battle. Again we weighed the giant and quickly released it. The battle with the larger peacock was not as exciting or long lasting as the one with the previous fish. Obviously, hook placement can have a significant impact on the battle with a big fish!

Where the hooks penetrate the peacock also has a lot to do with the condition of the lure after the battle. A giant peacock with two trebles in its mouth can use leverage and "jaw power" to bend or pull out the beefiest of hooks. When I landed the 16-pounder, it had straightened out one of the lure's middle 4/0 extra-strength treble hook points and completely pulled out the big rear treble hook, which was still embedded in its mouth. What awesome power they have!

The Nitro bass boats at the Rio Negro Lodge are the Amazon's most comfortable fishing machines.

Doubling Up On The Giant River

We took another five peacocks up to 12 pounds from that "sweet spot" in a lagoon just off Brazil's Rio Negro. The waterway there offers some of the most exciting peacock bass fishing in the tropics. The river itself is the largest of the dozen major tributaries of the mighty Amazon River. Encompassing an archipelago of hundreds of large islands, backwater sloughs, lagoons, creeks and low-water lakes, the Rio Negro spreads 15 miles wide in places.

There are many "sweet spots" in the area. Fishing another one later that day, we caught five peacocks that ranged from 6 to 11 pounds. All were taken on our topwater plugs from beside one small flooded bush. One of those fish was particularly memorable. The 9-pounder shot out of the brush and up through the surface, grabbing the plug, and then "flew" 10 feet laterally before crashing back down into the water.

Our eyes widened and mouths gaped open in awe at the aerobatics. I leaned back on the rod and felt the fish that had set the hook itself so energetically. After such a performance, I felt especially good in releasing it.

The fishing action when after peacocks is often exciting, and "doubles" often enter into the picture. On the first day of the trip, my partner and I caught 9-pound and 11-pound peacocks on parallel casts.

On the following day, I hooked one of a school of 6- to 7-pound peacock bass, and before I got it to the boat, Jensen hooked one of its classmates. The guide netted my fish and swung around to prepare to net my partner's. I quickly laid down my rod and grabbed another, flipping another Woodchopper topwater near Jensen's struggling fish. I had an

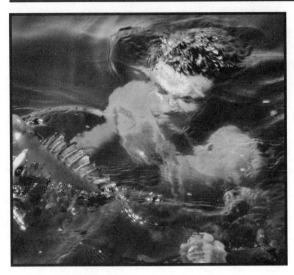

Most of the experienced guides will go overboard after a giant peacock, and they usually get the fish and your plug back. Another "teener" comes aboard, the hard way!

immediate strike from one of the followers, and our guide slid the net under my partner's fish and then mine to complete the "triple".

You can imagine the tangle of big tail-spinner lures, line, net and three big very lively peacock bass!

Topwater-hungry giants that live in the black-clear waters of the Rio Negro can make any trip exciting and memorable. Bass anglers can get spoiled easily in the jungle. But keep in mind that it is jungle! You literally have to pull your own weight.

Cutting Through The Jungle

On several occasions, my native guide has steered the fiberglass bass boat into a wooded pocket that seemingly ended abruptly. There, he quickly moves to the bow and uses his machete to clear a narrow passageway for our entry into a hidden lagoon. He cuts vines and chops limbs in the brushy tunnel while my partner and I pull and push the boat forward in the canopied darkness.

We usually emerge over an entanglement of fallen limbs into the forest-surrounded water hole. That's not always true though. On my most recent trip to the area, my guide, partner Jim Wise and I worked our way through an extremely shallow, 10-foot wide creek full of tangles. A second boat followed and we helped to lift, push and pull the two vessels over fallen trees and limbs that lay around each bend. We felt we were in the middle of an Indiana Jones adventure searching for the lost temple of giant peacock!

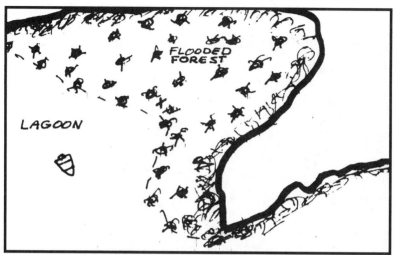

Figure 7 - Small, tree-flooded coves often exist in Rio Negro lagoons and backwaters. Usually, the biggest fish will be concentrated along the treeline. The most productive casts for big fish will be those between the trunks in the deepest water. Once a strike occurs, often many fish can be taken from that particular spot. This is one "sweet spot" that I found on my recent trip. Lesson: Fish between the outermost trees in the deepest water for the biggest peacocks. Once fish are contacted, pound the spot hard!

After more than an hour of work, mostly through our guides' efforts, we reached the mouth of the lagoon. Two inches of water over a 40-foot long sandbar prohibited our boat from entering the very deep lagoon.

Needless to say, we were disappointed. Jim and I waded off the bar to make a few casts. An 11 pounder exploded on my topwater plug and Jim was fast to an 8 pounder on his second cast. The two fish so accessible from the only open area along the bank to wade further added to our disappointment about not being able to get the boat into the lake.

The often mirror-smooth lagoons like that one are usually very productive. They have probably not been fished for several months. Fishing the edges of a wall of trees with laydowns and overhanging limbs from a boat often yields the biggest fish. There are plenty of such spots off the Rio Negro and guides from the Rio Negro Lodge know where they are.

F lorida angler Dave Burkhardt caught this "teener" from a cast down the middle of a blackwater lagoon. Later in the week, he garnered a 21 pounder.

Storming Giants And Laydowns

The "chug-and-pause" retrieve was sending off the right cadence to attract a monster peacock bass. The giant, modified Woodchopper was cutting a path along a canopied shoreline against a high bank when a giant fish exploded on it. A couple of buckets full of water blew out of the "hole" onto the bank, as I hung on for dear life.

As an approaching storm appeared on the horizon above the trees, the monster put up a great fight. It pulled drag, leaped above the surface three times and circled the boat. The big topwater plug firmly attached between its lips held, and I worked it near the boat as the skies darkened. The fish made two more strong surges toward a big laydown but never quite made it. I slowly recovered line and moved the peacock away from the entanglement before it succumbed to the waiting net.

My giant fish weighed 20 ½ pounds on our BogaGrip scales. I had hoped to get several pictures of the giant once I landed it, but it started to pour rain within a few seconds. I quickly grabbed my camera and had my fishing partner, Ken Graves, take a couple of quick snapshots. We then released the fish. While that was going on, Ken tossed in behind my fish, hoping for a second giant. He also had a hard strike and set the hook into a peacock. My partner, of Pelham, AL, landed a 15 pounder, while in a nearby boat, friends Dave Burkhardt of Clermont, FL and John Ranchoff, of Fairview Park, OH, caught 21 and 14 pounders, respectively.

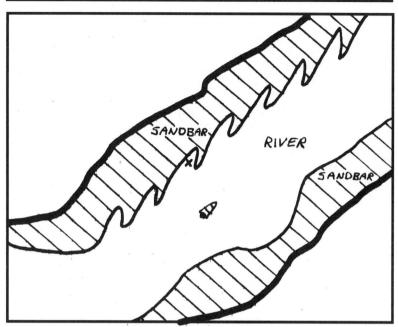

Figure 8 – At low water, larger tributaries, like the Negro, often have areas of sand buildup that resembles "waves" from above. A series of pockets and points lie along some of these sandbars, and when depth of three foot or more is present, then larger fish may be also. This low water river pattern is very productive and for a few weeks can yield numerous 8 to 12 pound fish. Then when the majority of nearby lagoons have "dried up," look for "teeners" to occupy such spots. Lesson: When waters are very low and lagoons are shallow, work on the deep pockets in the rolling topography of long river sandbars!

We were focusing on the lagoons and lakes near the luxurious Rio Negro Lodge on the banks of the Brazilian river with the same moniker. The waterway near the lodge offers some of the most exciting giant peacock bass action in South America. The river itself is the largest of the dozen major tributaries of the mighty Amazon River. Encompassing an archipelago of hundreds of large islands, backwater sloughs, lagoons, creeks and low-water lakes, the Rio Negro spreads 15 miles wide in places and is full of 20-pounders.

The Rio Negro Lodge, 60 miles northwest of Barcelos, is the nicest land-based facility in the Amazon jungle.

Sizeable Season Stats

In the 2001-2002 fishing season which spans from October through March, Amazon Tour's detailed logs reveal that guests at their Rio Negro Lodge and aboard their sister operation, the Amazon Queen riverboat caught 374 peacocks weighing 20 pounds or better in those waters. In fact, the IGFA all-tackle record peacock bass was caught by one of Marsteller's customers about 20 minutes from the site of the lodge. The 27-pounder was caught a few years ago.

The topwater-hungry giants that live in the black-clear waters of the Rio Negro can make any trip exciting and memorable. On my last trip to the lodge, 14 anglers caught 12 peacocks over 20 pounds. I was fortunate enough to land the 20 pounder mentioned earlier and several others over 10. On the trip before that one, over 2,000 peacocks were caught and released by my group during the week, and almost 400 of them were 10 pounds or better! I again caught a 20 pounder on that trip.

My 20's and most of the other behemoths were taken on giant Luhr-Jensen topwater plugs, specifically the Magnum Woodchopper. The "clown-pattern" (painted yellow with red and black dots), "fire tiger", "peacock bass", "red and white", "perch" and "black with orange belly" versions all produced big peacocks.

One on my last trip to the lodge stands out in my mind. I had cast my Woodchopper over an extended tree branch about 15 feet off the water's surface. Dave Burkhardt, my partner that morning, chuckled at my predicament. As I always do, I jiggled the surface plug slowly to try to entice any piscatorial eyes beneath it. The chopper danced like a puppet until a three-pound butterfly peacock exploded on it. The fish yanked the line off the branch and fought all the way to the boat. We both laughed at the circumstances.

Most of the "teeners" of the Rio Negro are tough characters, and this one that almost destroyed the author's topwater plug was no exception.

What is needed after a 10-hour day of tossing 7-inch long, 1 1/2 ounce topwater plugs and battling big peacock averaging 7 or 8 pounds each, is a comfortable respite. Marsteller's Rio Negro Lodge, completed in 1998, provides that. It lies on the southern bank of the river about 60 miles west north west of Barcelos, the "tropical fish capital of the world". Many of the pretty exotic fish at the aquarium shop are often captured and shipped from this region of the Amazon watershed. Guess what the area's peacock bass forage on?

Luxury Lodge And Boats

The accommodations are the finest offered by any peacock operation in South America that this writer has visited in over 50 trips to that part of the world. Tucked into the rainforest are air conditioned guest cabins and an air conditioned, 5,000 square foot central lodge with dining, relaxation and recreation lounge, bar area an office, a tackle area, a giant aquarium and a gift shop area. The main building has exposed-beam ceilings and large glass windows that overlook an expansive grass area. The cabins all have open-beam ceilings and large windows that look out over the Rio Negro. Trees in front of the cabins are thinned for guests to enjoy a partial view of the river, but are dense enough for privacy from the passing boats. Hardwood trees climbing 200 feet into the sky are wrapped by native vines and surrounded by a variety of flowering foliage.

The operation's 17-foot Nitro bass boats with 90 hp outboards pick up the anglers each morning at the shoreside dock and whisk them off to often mirror-smooth lagoons. The lodge is located in the heart of the prime fishery and the guides have lots of water to fish. Some of the better areas are the Rio Cuiuni, Rio Itu, Rio Ariraha, Rio Erere and Rio Padauari. There are hundreds of lagoons off those tributaries and the main Rio Negro. As an option, guests can also "fly out" to isolated, land-locked lagoons on either a floatplane or a helicopter that Marsteller owns.

I love big peacocks, and they love the Rio Negro, which has for several years yielded more giants over 20 pounds than any other watershed in the Amazonas region of Brazil. There are plenty of giant peacocks there for all of us!

Amazon Tour Community Access

Marsteller's Amazon Tours has been in business longer than any other Brazilian peacock bass operation. For over ten years, he has booked trips on the renowned Amazon Queen, and for the past five years at the Rio Negro Lodge.

While peacock bass fishing is the main interest of his guests, Marsteller's is to give back to the community he loves. His Rio Negro Foundation was set up to provide the people of the Amazon region with a better, brighter future. They have built a school, a medical clinic with full time doctor from the United States and a dental clinic with visiting American dentists for the employees of the lodge and the indigenous people in the vicinity. A Research Center at the lodge conducts studies of flora and fauna in the remote area.

Visitors with a passport and visa fly into Manaus from Miami and then take a charter flight to Barcelos where boat transfers are made to the Rio Negro Lodge. For more information on the Rio Negro Lodge, the Amazon Queen or the new Araca River Lodge, contact Amazon Tours at P.O. Box 3106, Coppell, TX 75019; email usa@peacockbassfishing.com; or phone (972) 304-1656.

Chapter 7

BEAUTIFUL MOUNTAIN PEACOCK!

Wild Waters At Belo Monte Fishing Lodge Offer Unique Peacock Species

As our guide, Mana, used the electric motor to pull our boat into a flat pool off the main channel rapids, I paused to admire the scenic waterway. My partner went ahead and cast to one of the outlet chutes and hooked a small peacock. The activity was expected; almost all the side pools and eddies along the current-swept river had several fish in them.

When my first cast beyond a large rock outcropping in the relatively shallow pool landed, I started cranking the Krocodile spoon. On the third crank, a "fishy" freight train slammed the bait and ripped through the 25-yard wide pool. I hung on and prayed that the rock outcropping that was prevalent throughout most all of the pools and side channels of the Xingu would not slice my very taut line.

The power of the fish was awesome; large river peacocks seem to exhibit superior power and endurance to those of similar size in lagoons. I was impressed by this peacock, which was a shade less than 9 pounds. It gave me a battle I could not easily forget. It was my largest Xingu River fish of the week, and the setting could not have been more memorable.

The Xingu is a riverbed of rocks protected by rocky outcropping all along its meandering course. Only at high water does the waterscape change drastically as the water moves into the edges of the forest and amongst the trees. The river in the Belo Monte area makes U-turns, hard right-angle turns and is split by islands, boulders and outcroppings everywhere. The pools lie below rapids, falls and other rock masses. In some situations, part of the stream shoots off in one direction, running through the forest and then reenters the main course of the river a mile away, after it tumbles down a rock-filled gully.

T   *he strong peacocks in the craggy Xingu River are often in the eddies
     and rocky coves off the main channels. While there are numerous
peacocks in these waters, they seldom grow larger than 10 pounds. Many
other exotics also keep an angler very busy here.*

Channeling The Peacock Fishing

The best fishing for peacocks, which seldom reach 10 pounds in the
Xingu, may be found in the quiet lagoon waters or in the deep pools with
slow currents or in the eddies adjacent large, river-lining boulders that
block substantial currents. In this region of the Xingu, there are only a
few lagoons that are surrounded by forests; others are surrounded by
rocks of various sizes. Fishing from some of the rocky islands can also
be productive, particularly for fly fishermen.

We were in one of the many side channels of the river in the
archipelago area south and east of Altamira, Brazil. The large pool had
small mountains jutting into the skies on two sides, ribbons of fast water
surrounding this pool, rocky islands everywhere, and even sharp sloping
sandbars at some of their edges. The blue-green clear waters swept over
small waterfalls, forming rapids and white water, and their turbulence
throughout the side channels was ever-changing. The shorelines were
composed of small rocks, large boulders, craggy volcanic rocks and
smooth river rock.

Ian Sulocki shows off his six-pound "freckled" golden peacock. The unique, beautiful fish are endemic to the Xingu watershed. The Brazilian writer/angler often fishes the Amazon region.

The Scenic Frecks and 10-Bars

While the scenery in this portion of the Xingu River basin is unsurpassed in the rainforest, so also is the beauty of the peacock bass varieties. A couple of species found here don't seem to resemble those in the rest of the Amazon watershed. One of the prettiest is the golden-yellow peacock, which has very tiny specks of black on its sides. I call it a "freckled" golden peacock, not to be confused with the more common speckled peacock that is found throughout the Amazon.

The second unusual peacock is the 10-bar, a dark green fish which may have anywhere between 5 and 10 vertical bars varying from gray to faint black on each side. I have not seen this fish in other areas of Brazil that I've fished. The third type of peacock in the area was a speckled peacock that was very dark in nature. The freckled golden peacock is found throughout the Xingu, and I had caught several of them a few years ago when fishing several hundred miles upstream on the same river. Add

The beautiful waters of the Xingu offer waterscapes with boulders, waterfalls and clear waters, similar to many trout and/or smallmouth streams in the states. Most of the peacocks are caught in the slower waters just out of the current.

to the unique colorations of the peacock the big variety of fish that swim in these areas, and you have some exciting fishing.

On this particular trip I was fishing with Ian Sulocki, co-owner of High Hook Fishing Tours. Ian cast his lure between two giant boulders and had a strike on his topwater plug, but the fish missed it. I quickly tossed a 1-ounce vibrating bait to the spot of attack and immediately hooked up with a 6 pounder.

Vigorous Variety Values

While I caught about 40 to 50 fish per day, generally 15 to 20 were peacocks and the rest were piranha up to 4 ½ pounds, bicuda up to about 6 pounds, jacunda, a couple of species of pacu, and an occasional trieda. Members of our fishing group also fished for and caught 3 species of catfish. Had I been using smaller lures, I am convinced that I could have probably doubled the production of both peacocks and other species. And, while the peacock offers more than enough challenge, it is very exciting to see the variety of fish that anglers can catch in this watershed.

The Xingu is not a giant fish area. In fact, in four days, I caught several five and six pounders and 5 peacocks between 7 and 8 ½ pounds. I used small lures such as lipless cranks, spoons and a topwater Jerk'n Sam. The lures are very effective around the waterfalls, rapid eddies and pools in the rocks and boulders. Many rocky islands and swirling currents provided eddies to throw at. One of my 6 pounders came from a rocky landlocked lake that had a volcanic rock-strewn landscape to walk along to reach the shore.

*L*arry examines an eight-pound "freckled" golden peacock that fell for a vibrating plug. Quiet pools all along the Xingu harbor many strong mid-size peacock bass. Rocks and sand beaches block current in the prime spots.

Irregular Shoreline/Active Peacocks

On most days, shallow spots and those with current held few fish. At other times, deeper haunts off irregular shores held active fish that struck one out of every 6 to 10 of our casts. White sand beaches with quick drops highlighted some banks that tended to be mostly rocky. Agent Scott Swanson and a friend caught 60 peacocks to 9 pounds one day and 35 on another.

Catfishermen in our group, including Brazilian Rene Von der Kley, caught 10 catfish, mostly redtails, up to 40 pounds during the week. One 60-pound redtail was brought to the boat and then after a couple of minutes of thrashing off the gunwale, spit out the hook. The anglers then caught 3 more barbado catfish of 12 to 15 pounds apiece on live and cut piranha bait. They tossed the bait with 7/0 circle hooks and 3 to 4 ounces of weights to the edge of the current lines that were over 100 foot deep and let it go to the bottom

Flavio Ferreira, of Rio de Janeiro, has caught numerous golden peacocks from the Xingu waters below the Belo Monte Lodge. His favorite plugs are shallow-running minnowbaits.

"Smokey Falls" or Cachorro Fumoito, is a drop of about 10 feet that is a beautiful backdrop for fishing the numerous pools nearby. It was in one of them when one of the most interesting things of the week happened. A small jacunda had followed my partner, Scott's topwater plug right to the boat, when at the last moment, a giant peacock appeared from nowhere and engulfed the jacunda – before it could strike the plug. What a memory.

Experienced Summer Angling

Ian Sulocki has fished the area 7 times previously and has caught peacocks up to 9 pounds, redtail up to 50 pounds, and bicuda up to 5 pounds. The bicudas hang out in the current near the edges, as do the piranha. Ian has seen trieda up to 20 pounds hanging out in some of the land-locked lagoons off the Xingu. They are most available during the summer and fall when waters in northeast Brazil are lowest. Payara up to 30 pounds swim below the big waterfalls in the river. Payara in the area are more active at dusk, and for those wanting to use live bait, the slender peau is a great one.

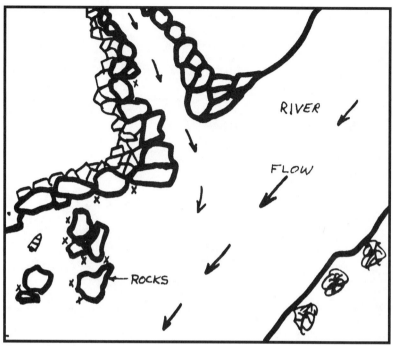

Figure 9 – The Xingu River has numerous islands and small tributaries entering and leaving the main channels. While a huge variety of fish exist all over the waterway, most peacocks are taken from the quieter waters just out of the strong currents. The golden peacock are positioned tighter to the banks and behind more boulder "blocks" than they are in the rest of the Amazon (which has minimal current flow). Anglers should make very accurate casts to all eddies, pockets, coves, rock islands and narrow passageways between boulders to catch the super-powered, larger peacocks. Lesson: Fish "slack" water over 4-foot in depth that lies adjacent to large boulders or other current blocking structure/ topography.

The pacu seringa, which eats the fruit of the rubber tree, is the largest species of pacu, and it grows to 9 or 10 pounds. They are caught in the winter months on mussels or tiny crabs or worms. The other three species of pacu are curuaued, white and cadete, which is a small pacu that is primarily caught and used for catfish bait. Freshwater corvina are caught when the Xingu is full between February and June.

*T*he Belo Monte Lodge is a beautiful facility about 2-hours drive from Altimira that sits high atop a small "mountain" overlooking miles of the Xingu River.

Giant piraiba and jau catfish are normally caught in February through April when waters are high and the fish can swim around in deep waters everywhere. The redtail, surubim and palmbeto catfish are caught year around. The barbado catfish world record was taken from the Xingu and weighed 17 pounds. The best fishing for the biggest catfish, according to Ian, is in the deep river holes early in the morning and just after sunset around the dark moon phase. Whole piranha, peau, and payara are often used for bait when after the big cats.

Hilltop Perch With Beautiful View

The 2-story tall Belo Monte Lodge is on the highest hill in the area, and anglers on most parts of the river within 30 minutes run or 4 or 5 miles away, can easily see the massive structure. The dining room and sofa-abundant game room with giant Satellite TV is the centerpiece of Claudomiro Gomes' lodge. There are 8 comfortable air-conditioned bedrooms with private showers and telephones. The lodge serves chicken, beef and fish almost every night and they make great fries. The have salads and vegetables, rice, a desert and pasta each night.

The lodge on the hilltop overlooking the archipelago of perhaps 100 islands several hundred feet below, has only been open for just a year, but clients have caught payara up to 20 pounds and redtail catfish up to 60 pounds, peacocks up to 9 pounds and pacu of 7 pounds. The peacock is the main fish on the river, according to Ian. All of the lodge's guides are from the area and worked as commercial fishermen prior to the opening of the sportfishing facility. The fishery now is exclusively catch-and-release, with the exception of a couple of small fish for lodge dining purposes.

They are developing a runway for landing charter aircraft to improve logistics. The lodge is just two hours by air from Manaus or 1 ½ hours from Belem. They also plan on putting boats in a couple of the landlocked lakes so that anglers can just walk through the jungle with his gear and get aboard.

Prime time to fish this area is the summer months. My trip was in August. The animal and bird life of the Amazon was present. I saw my first Amazon deer on a sandy riverbank there, and the rare arratta azul or blue macaws flew over several times. They have a unique sound, which is a lower pitch in their calls. We saw many more yellow macaws and heard some toucans also.

Visitors fly into Belem and change planes to access Altamira. While in Belem, try the Estacao do Docas restaurant area for great ambiance and food if you have time. For information, contact Flavio Ferreira, Director of Business Development or Ian Sulocki, Director of Operations of High Hook Fishing Tours at R. Teofilo Otoni, 135, sala 401, 20090-080, Rio de Janeiro RJ Brazil, phone 011-5521-2516-9622 or email highhook@transpacific.com.br.

Chapter 8

UPROAR ON THE UNINI RIVER

Giant Peacocks May Yank You Out Of The Boat!

I lofted my giant Amazon Ripper toward the laydown just off the near shore of the narrow lagoon. The plug was mid-way toward its landing when a big fish blew up the water's surface some 100 yards away as it chased 3/4 pound baitfish against the opposite shore. The guide instinctively started to swing the stern of the boat with the electric to ready us for the chase after that feeding fish. My surface plug landed about 20 feet off the sharp dropping bank as the boat slowly began to move away.

Popping it twice, I was ready to reel it in quickly and prepare myself for a long cast at the fish that had given its location away just 10 seconds earlier. I didn't have a chance. A giant peacock exploded on my plug and then fired its afterburners and exploded away. If that sounds like a lot of "explosions", well, there is just no other adjective to describe this action!

The fish ripped the rod from my hand and I watched it fly off and slowly start to sink. My guide, my partner and I all quickly grabbed rods to try to snag the sinking rod and reel. I was very lucky. Initially, the fish had bolted 10 feet toward the bank, but then it turned and headed for deep water away from the brush pile. That slowed the acceleration of the rod away from me in the bow of the boat, and my guide Sabastiao Brito was able to get one of my backup rods under it.

I jumped to the stern of our aluminum fishing boat and grabbed the rod handle as he flipped it to the surface. I was happy to save my $450 outfit but was elated that the fish was still on. I grabbed the wet rod with two hands as the peacock powered its way down the small lagoon. It reversed course and jumped three feet out of the water. I hung on as it again jetted away, back toward the laydowns.

The author's 24 ½ pounder ripped the rod and reel from his hands in his initial explosion on the Amazon Ripper topwater plug. Albeit embarrassing, Larry quickly grabbed the outfit as it was sinking into the depths to salvage the experience and reel in the monster!

"That's a good fish," my partner Ruede Wheeler shouted. The experienced angler would know. He had caught a 19-1/2 pounder two days earlier and his largest ever, a 23-1/2 pounder the day before in the same lagoon. I had been "snake bit" the first four days of the trip failing to catch a peacock over about 12 pounds, but I knew this one was over 20.

I leaned back with all I could on my 7-foot rod redirecting the fish away from the obstructions. It jumped twice more before I could work it

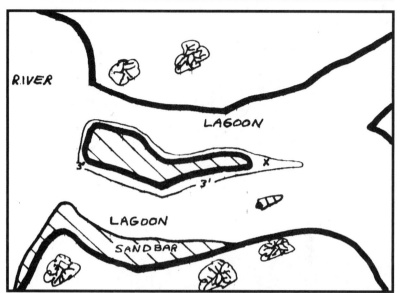

Figure 10 – A large lagoon just off the lower Rio Unini had a high sandbar extending from the entrance well into the lake where it tapered into a submerged point. The extended point off the inside portion of the lagoon bar (which had relatively deep water adjacent along it) was a classic spot for "teeners". My second cast to the spot found a mad giant ready to do battle. Lesson: Learn the classic spots and fish them. Submerged points off sand banks should be fished thoroughly along their length until they descend deeper than five feet!

close to the boat. Sabastiao tried unsuccessfully to scoop it up 3 times, and my heart sank 3 times when the fish powered away from the big net. On the fourth attempt, I kept the bass' head up and into the net it went. The monster was mine.

Rod Overboard Action And Reaction

Sebastiao quickly unhooked the fish and weighed it. The 24-1/2 pounder was my largest ever (at that time) in some 30 trips to Brazil after the ultimate freshwater fish. We measured it at 34 inches and a 22-inch girth and then, for good measure, confirmed the weight on another set of scales. After a few pictures, we released the giant and watched it swim away in good shape. High 5's were in order, and we all three laughed as we recalled the rod overboard ordeal.

Gu i d e Sabastiao Brito curls the 44-½ pound "double" that the author (with a 25 pounder) and Ruede Wheeler (with a 19 ½ pounder) caught from the same productive spot. It is the largest the author and his partner have ever taken to date.

Never before had any fish, even a peacock bass, jerked the rod from my hands. I have caught several hundred big fish of various species in the 20 to 40 pound range on the same tackle without losing my grasp of the

Texan Ruede Wheeler shows off one of his 22-pounders that slammed a Woodchopper in one of the blackwater lagoons off the Unini.

rod. Heck, I have caught numerous tarpon between 80 and 120 pounds on the same equipment without such an embarrassment. I felt foolish.

I had heard numerous stories in the Amazon about anglers having their rods jerked from their hands by big peacock, but I discounted the possibility of an avid angler like myself with extensive experience catching giant peacock bass living such an occurrence. I was wrong, and I am humbled. I had never said that it couldn't happen to me, just that it was a slim possibility. The 24-1/2 pound "keg of dynamite" from Brazil's Unini River straightened out my thinking.

Trolling Topwaters For Giants

Ruede and I were fishing a large black-water lagoon just off the river that offered more than a dozen false channels, some of which were 1/2 mile long. Rain showers were a part of our daily experience and the river was rising each day and turning more turbid. While the river turned to

*L*arry's 25-pounder is his personal best to date, but like many other avid anglers, he is after an even larger one. This one exploded on a modified orange and black Amazon Ripper (one with a third set of trebles added).

a muddy-looking brown color, some lagoons remained relatively undisturbed with the prime black-clear waters.

The day before, after casting about four hours, we were trolling our 7-inch long topwater Woodchoppers along one of the points in the big maze of a lagoon when a giant exploded on Ruede's black and orange version. The 23 1/2 pounder headed straight toward the wooded shoreline, stripping my partner's braided line all the way to the few feet of monofilament backing on the spool. Watching the line disappear, Ruede shouted at Sabastiao to reverse the engine, which the Brazilian guide had already done.

It was the moment of truth with the only the arbor knot maintaining the connection with the big fish. Suddenly, the boat gained traction in the reverse mode and the fish swam into a submerged tree trunk where one of the loose treble hooks snagged its root. Ruede was then able to put line back on his spool as the boat headed toward the hung-up fish, visible in about 3 feet of water. Such entanglements are the cause of a lot of lost fish, but my partner was lucky.

As we approached, the fish saw the boat and bolted toward deep water, tearing the plug's hook from the trunk. The giant, 33 inches long with a 21-inch girth, was still attached to the plug! Ruede then fought the fish with a partially full spool of line in open water and eventually won the battle. It was his largest peacock in five trips with operator River Plate

Big baits are usually effective for big fish, and that is never truer than with peacock bass. The 6 ½- inch-long Woodchopper often calls 20-pound-plus fish with big mouths into an area for a "snack."

Anglers and the trophy of his very productive big fish week. He also caught three 19 1/2 pounders, and fish of 21, 22 and 22 1/2 pounds. His previous personal best was 21 pounds.

Locating A Monstrous Blackwater "Double"

My big 24 1/2 pounder was my personal best for only one day. On the following day, Ruede and I ventured an hour up river in search of new water with good quality and visibility. After several days of intermittent rain, many of the lagoons with large mouths into the river were turning turbid. The water level of the Unini had risen a couple of feet over the week, and finding the perfect lagoon waters was becoming difficult. We went into 3 brown-water lagoons off the river before Sabastiao snaked our 18 foot-long boat through a short, twisting creek mouth with overgrown foliage.

We ducked under a fallen tree and pushed back brush to work the boat through the shallow channel. Clinging vines whipped us from above and bushes scrapped our fishing equipment and us as we passed. Finally, it opened up into a beautiful crescent shaped lagoon with dark, black-clear water. Fish were moving along both banks and in the middle. We caught 3 or 4 mid-size fish around 10 pounds each, before moving into big fish territory.

Sighting a big fish chasing bait near one shore we moved our boat to the action and loft our casts toward the disturbed water. On my second cast back to the same spot, a big peacock exploded on my orange and black Big Game Ripper. It powered away pulling off line from a tightened drag. Two minutes into the fight, I had a modicum of control when it shot skyward to fully reveal itself.

"Grande," I said to my partner as I glanced toward Ruede who was not even looking at my fish. He was busy with a fish of his own. A follow-up cast to the area where I had hooked up met with success for him, and he, too, had his hands full.

Both big fish were brought to the net at the same time and Sabastiao netted them. My fish was truly a giant, weighing 25 pounds even. Ruede's peacock was certainly not a baby at 19 1/2 pounds. The pair weighing a total of 44 1/2 pounds was the largest peacock "double" that I have ever heard of. Several years ago, I and another friend had taken two peacocks that weighed 39 pounds even. Ruede, a dentist from LaPorte, Texas, wasn't through.

Fishing Tactics For Bubbles And Mid-Lake Haunts

Within 30 feet of that spot on his third cast, my partner hooked and landed a 22 1/2 pounder. I caught and released a 20 1/2 pounder later in another lagoon to cap off a very great day.

The fishing during the week on the Unini was decent in terms of numbers, but it was excellent for giant 20-plus pound peacocks. While the five active anglers in our fly-in barge camp operation landed over 300 peacock, 10 were over 20 pounds. Ruede, of LaPorte, TX, caught 4 over 20 pounds and I captured 3, including the two largest.

Avid anglers Paul Engel of Naples, FL and Greg Hochstetter of Jupiter, FL caught a total of 3 fish over 20 pounds during the week. Our group also caught 29 teeners, and Ruede had the most, 9 of them.

Most of our fish were taken from a variety of places. Backs of lagoons in shallow flooded timber were productive areas for a couple of days. Sand bars adjacent deep water held big fish a couple of days, and laydowns proved prime spots a few times.

Most big peacock were taken 30 or 40 feet off the shoreline, and some mid-lake catches were enticed by casting to visible schools of fry on the surface of a quiet lagoon. The technique of casting to "bubbles" or the "ball" of fry as they swim slowly along and dimple the surface is effective for the two parents, which are usually swimming beneath their brood.

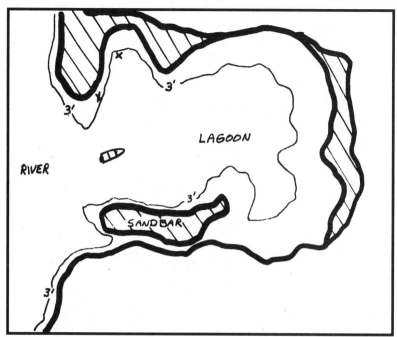

Figure 11 – One of the most attractive targets for giant peacock bass in a lagoon is a large sandbar with adjacent deep water. Fish are often contacted around such prime spots and it is not wise to pass up such habitat. In a lagoon like this, my partner and I took two 20-pounders off the opposite bank. One was near the point formed by the mouth of the lagoon and river and the other was in the first "pocket" just off that point. A deep-water swing-in allowed the big fish roaming water. Lesson: Don't focus all your attention on one very prominent structure to the exclusion of other typical, classic big fish spots that also offer depth.

They will blast a lure tossed near in an instinctive reflex mode. Bret Myers of Ft. Worth, TX also caught some teeners up to 17 ½ pounds fishing mid-lake regions and fry balls.

Lure Choice And Productive Modification

We also threw our big topwaters at feeding fish that were blowing up the surface while chasing bait. The Luhr-Jensen Big Game, Single Prop Woodchoppers were the most effective lures most of the week. While a few of the big fish were taken on Fire Tiger models, the orange and black color scheme proved to be the top peacock attractor. Magnum Amazon Rippers, also made by Luhr-Jensen, were a distant second in terms of lure productivity. My largest fish of the week came on a modified 6 1/2-inch long Ripper. I had added a third treble hook and removed one of the two tail spinners.

Submerged baits that typically do well, such as the Pet spoon, Krocodile spoon, and several varieties of minnow baits, were not very effective under the existing conditions. It was a "topwater week" for the most part, but not all attractions proved successful. One of the most vivid images from the week was a 12 pounder that come up under the plug and jumped out of the water 3 foot in the air, landing some 10 foot laterally on its tail at reentry. The fish, as in a slow-motion video, remained vertical with mouth agape and lure between its lips for the full 4 seconds or so of its flight. When it crashed back into the water, the peacock simply opened its mouth and released the lure.

Another great memory was a 22 pounder that exploded on Ruede's big Woodchopper and jetted off under a 30-foot wide tree that hung off the nearby bank at about a foot above the surface. There was no way to get the boat under the tree and chase the fish which had bulled on down the bank another 50 feet before becoming temporarily entangled in some brush. So, Sabastiao went around the tree, as my partner let out line while keeping a taunt connection to the fish. The guide then grabbed the braid and hand-lined the tired, giant fish to the net.

On The Move Camping And Scenery

Between hook-ups, there were plenty of distractions. In some areas, freshwater dolphin rolled on the surface of the river or lagoon. Caiman slid off the banks and disappeared into the depths in a few lagoons and the skies overhead were always busy. Macaws and papagaios (green parrots) were almost hourly sightings, and toucans and pato ducks added color and uniqueness to the "aeroscape". During a shoreside lunch break one day, a river otter, locally called "lantra", popped up on a log just 20 feet away from our boat and curiously viewed us in our "feeding" mode.

The River Plate Anglers Safari Camp is a spacious screen house lodge with separate dining and lounge areas. Each 10 foot wide by 15 foot long cabin barge or screened-in bungalow has two beds, a toilet and shower combination, a sink, table reading lamps and cooling fans over the beds. Generators provide power for cooking and recharging batteries that handle bungalow lighting, fans and water pumps and electric trolling motors on the fishing boats. Each evening, after a swim in the

River Plate Anglers Safari camps accommodate anglers in 10-foot wide by 15-foot long cabin barges that are relocated each day while anglers are off fishing.

river, our group of anglers enjoyed cocktails and hot hors d'oeuvres while watching the sunset and recounting daily conquests and failures.

During our November week on the Unini, our camp moved upriver on three different days, totaling about 25 miles during the week. The moves keep the numerous lagoon fishing waters ever changing. The camp management and staff would break camp mid-morning, hook up all the barge components, and then tow them to another expansive sandbar. In the afternoon, the individual bungalows are once again spread out along the beach for some privacy.

The Amazon Peacock Bass Safari by River Plate Anglers offers anglers the very best access a variety of the most remote waters holding the biggest fish in the Amazon. To find out more, contact booking agent J.W. Smith of Rod & Gun Resources, 206 Ranch House Rd., Kerrville, TX 78028; Phone (800) 211-4753; FAX (830) 792-6807; e-mail: venture@rodgunresources.com or visit their website at www.rodgunresources.com.

After dark, we fall asleep listening to croaking frogs and sounds of other nocturnal creatures. We dream of the next giant peacock bass that will dare try to jerk the rod from our hands. That's scary, but it doesn't have to be a nightmare!

Chapter 9

VICTORIOUS VOYAGE UP THE NEGRO

Cruise And Fish The Big Black River In Luxury

The spot was ideal for big peacock. A brushy, quick-dropping right-angle point bordered it on the right. On the left about 40 feet from the point were several giant, flooded hardwood trees that roughly defined a "cut" back into a large "feeding flat". My partner, Gary Laden, and I had fished the edge of the flat with its enticing deep blackwater for about 300 yards without success.

As we approached the "cut", I suggested to my partner that he cast to the left of center and I would take the right side, nearest the point. Our casts landed at about the same time, and a small four-pounder jumped on my topwater plug immediately. I brought it to the boat where guide "Banana" quickly grabbed it with the Boga. Gary's second cast to the left side of the same area about 25 feet off the largest flood tree on the cut's perimeter splashed down and he began his ripping cadence back to the boat.

On his fifth rip, a giant fish blew up on his Woodchopper, missing the hardware. Temporarily out of commission until Banana could get my smaller fish unhooked, I looked on in awe. My partner quickly shot another cast back to the spot and started to work his bait back to the boat. Banana finished his task releasing my fish and I quickly tossed my Big Game Woodchopper toward the middle of the cut.

Neither of us garnered a strike, so Gary switched to a diving minnowbait and we again fired our plugs back deeper into the opening. I twitched my Fire Tiger-painted topwater and a massive peacock exploded on it. The fish tore off toward the brushy point as I hung on and tried to turn it. Fortunately, the giant peacock turned at the edge of the

The author caught the big fish of the week, this beautiful 20-pounder from a "slough" going between a point and some flooded trees. The fish missed the first surface plug tossed his way and then waited for our third cast back to the spot.

brush without getting entangled and jetted back deeper into the cut pulling drag from my Morrum one-piece casting reel.

I had confidence in the smooth drag that I had cranked down to the max and in my 100 pound test braid, but a giant fish, if he gets into the nasty cover typical on the Rio Negro, can get off a number of ways, including breaking the line and/or lure. The peacock was in dangerous territory (a large, brushy laydown being a few feet away) and moving at-will almost freely against my heavy rod action leverage and the drag.

Putting some additional thumb "drag" on the spool, I stopped the fish, and it turned. At that point, some 10 or 12 seconds into the battle, Gary screamed for Banana to move our boat out away from the flooded timber and brushy point.

"Rapido, rapido," he commanded our guide pointing toward the middle of the lagoon. "Good Job. Good Job." Banana was paddling like

Voyager owner Iomar Oliveira and his wife Linete are both avid fisher-people. They also enjoy visiting with the anglers aboard the yacht.

crazy, and I was still hanging on to a brute that then took to the air before charging off in another direction.

Taking a breath, Gary rooted me on, "Good Job Larry. Nice going. You got him now."

The action did move out into deeper water with minimal obstructions as the fish changed courses two or three more times, jumped twice again and then saw the boat. It again pulled drag for 10 feet or so, but it was far from worrisome entanglements around the flooded trees at that time. After a couple of laps around the boat in open water, the fish and I had our proverbial boatside brawl wherein the fish and I tug back and forth until the guide has a good shot at getting the net under the fish's head.

Landing Giants And "Early-Releasing" Them

Banana netted the monster with an entirely inadequate net – one that had the capacity to contain only about one half of my fish. Fortunately, he was able to lift the fish swiftly into the boat without it literally falling out of the net. We weighed the peacock on our certified scales at 20 pounds even and took several pictures before releasing the big fish.

My partner and I went on to catch 14 peacocks that day on Brazil's Rio Negro but we landed none even close to the giant in weight. I had on another very big fish that simply pulled off the hook and swam off. The peacock had exploded on my faithful surface lure, getting us all excited as such strikes typically do, but 5 seconds into the battle, it pulled free. On the positive side of such an experience, our adrenalin is pumped for another hour or so afterwards. We are increasingly alert for similar action!

Action in the afternoon slowed, but we headed back to our houseboat very satisfied with the day. We had boarded the Amazon Voyager II, a beautiful 108-foot long yacht, in Manaus at daylight a few days earlier and had boated up the Rio Negro in search of the prime areas for big peacock bass. We started fishing about 60 miles south of Barcelos and found the initial fishing very slow. Higher water in the lower Negro during our visit and the area's proximity to several villages along the river always impacts the quality fishing found on the giant river.

Brushy Mid-Lake Monsters Turn Quick

Fishing on our third day picked up, and booking agent "Wild Bill" Skinner and I caught about a dozen peacock. While my 12 pounder was the largest, I had on another monster.

The giant fish exploded on my big Woodchopper on my fourth cast down the middle of a small arm of a blackwater lagoon. It charged perpendicularly toward the nearest deepwater bank and a large, brushy laydown as I reeled frantically to keep it from the obstruction. It ran into the limbs and bulled further into the brush. I kept a taut line on the fish and felt it tugged and pulling drag further as my guide tried to paddle us toward the entanglement.

Wild Bill directed our guide to hurry over to the hung-up fish. As we approached, our guide stripped to his underwear and prepared to go overboard after the fish. It was still tugging, but I regained line on my spool with steady rod tension. I had forced the huge fish back up to a small limb and my guide grabbed one end to slowly raise it to the surface. Then, the fish turned quickly, and the tension was gone. Obviously, so was the fish.

We were all sick. The lure was removed from the small limb, and I examined it. The rear extra-strength eye screw holding the rear hook had been sheared off at its point of entry into the wooded plug. That must have been quite a fish to break a heavy-duty eye screw half way up the shaft. The plug was new that morning. I have seen the rear eye screws pull out of the wood body after much wear and abuse from peacocks, but this was the first time I have had a fish shear off the eye screw of a practically new plug!

Wild Bill Skinner is an avid angler who is at home pulling in giant largemouth in Mexico or peacocks in the Amazon. His favorite color topwater plug – Fire Tiger.

We frequently switched partners throughout the week, and I was joined by Randy Dornbusch of Lewisville, TX, booking agent Don Cutter of Weston, FL, Steve Schulte of St. Charles, MO and Amazon Voyager II owner/operator Iomar Oliveira and had very enjoyable fishing catching up to 15 per boat on the best day. While we didn't get too many big fish, most caught a "teener" during the week. Other anglers in our great group, Troy Jenkins of Austin, TX, fishing guide "Cooch" Cuccia of Oakley, CA, Dan Tracy of Chicago, IL and Karl Malik of Kensington, MD all caught some big peacocks.

Balls of Fry Tactics

Schulte and I had a productive day to finish off the week. We were fishing a lagoon area with scattered bushy tree "islands". The tiny,

*T*he *Voyager II yacht was our first class ride for the week on the Rio Negro. The Voyager I is slightly smaller but offers the same amenities.*

flooded "islands" held a few fish including a beautiful 13 pounder that jumped on my topwater cast about 25 feet off a point and put up an exciting battle. My partner and I also cast to several "balls" of fry. We were fortunate enough to hook 3 protective parents from the "fry" balls and all were quickly released.

What was very unusual about our "fry" ball catch was that only one of the fish we caught on our large topwater plugs were larger that five pounds. In my previous experience, I could almost guarantee any fish caught while protecting their fry would be over 10 pounds and often in the mid-teens or larger. The trip took place in early December and I believe the water was about 3 feet above optimum levels for spawning. We noticed a few beds in 2 to 3 feet of water.

Last Shot at Sundown

One of the highlights that day was the final "ball" we cast at near sundown. We were working through an area of flooded trees and small islands when the guide noticed two fry balls about10 feet apart in a narrow, quiet spot on one edge of the lagoon. Schulte, an extremely accurate caster, and I prepared to cast to them as our guide, "Jo-Jo" paddled quietly toward the fish. Schulte took the "ball" to the left and I, on his right, cast to the second "ball" on the right. Unfortunately, my partner's cast was a little long and tangled in a small flooded bush.

My cast landed on the fry and a big fish exploded on it. Schulte, who had worked his tail off trying for a giant, 13-pound or better fish that day, laughed as my fish took to the air. A couple of minutes later, I landed the

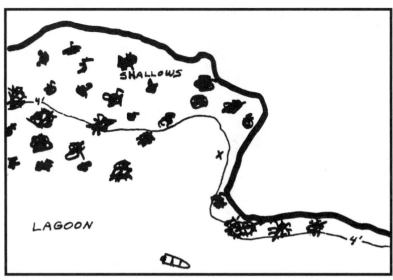

Figure 12 – The flooded forest where I caught my 20-pounder had an open-water "slough" separating it from a wooded point. The big fish depth of 4 feet was present adjacent the point and into the feeding flat about midway. Fishing the treeline and inside it for a 100-yards or so resulted in nothing. The water was 4 to 5 feet higher than normal and conditions tough, but the open-area slough was the perfect spot for a territorially positioned giant. My partner threw to the flooded forest side and I threw past the point to garner the strike. Lesson: Never past up a slough where deep water exists adjacent to a wooded point.

fat peacock. It only weighed 11 ½ pounds, so I was relieved that I hadn't lucked out and caught the fish he had been looking (a teener) for most of the day. While we landed 14 peacock bass that day, our average size was only around 6 or 7 pounds.

Very Comfortable Night Movements

Each night the beautiful Voyager would motor 30 miles or more to find unfished areas that might be more productive. We traveled as far as about 65 miles west northwest of Barcelos in the Amazonas state of Brazil. I only caught 28 peacocks in the tough-fishing five days with the two largest at 13 pounds and the giant 20-pounder (which along with another of the same size were big fish for the week aboard the Voyager), but I really enjoyed the trip.

*D*on Cutter shows off one of the hungry peacocks found in an oxbow lagoon off the Rio Negro.

The Voyager II has since been taken out of service, and today, Oliveira's primary boat is the Amazon Voyager I, which is an 84-foot river boat that accommodates 8 to 10 anglers. There are five very comfortable air-conditioned staterooms with complete private bathrooms. A satellite phone is available at a minimal charge for use by guests. Other amenities include a tackle shop, VCR, satellite TV, dining room, lounge room, two decks with tables and chairs. Oliveira, a bilingual Brazilian, makes sure that service aboard the Amazon Voyager I is excellent and that the fishing waters are prime.

Guests are flown via amphibious float planes to the boat positioned on a tributary somewhere in the Amazon upon their arrival at the international airport in Manaus. Fishing is from Brazilian-made 17-½ foot fishing boats with 50 hp outboards, electric trolling motors, live wells, raised casting decks and swivel seats. While the Voyager I is a relatively new operation at the time of this writing, most of their 6 guides have at least 5 years experience guiding for other Amazon sportfishing operations.

For more information on the Voyager I operation and trip availability, contact Don Cutter at Don Cutter's Peacockbasstrips.com, 1169 Tabor Lake Dr., Lexington, KY 40502; phone 888-626-2966; or e-mail peacockbasstrips@bellsouth.net or visit their website at www.amazonvoyager.com.

Chapter 10

NEXUS EXPLORATION OF THE UNKNOWN NHAMUNDA

Small Jon Boats Put Anglers Where Jungle Peacock Are Hiding

We fought off spiderwebs, clinging vines, sharp broken tree limbs and a few bugs as we slowly paddled through the overgrown creek. The 20-minute expedition through the almost inaccessible creek led to an isolated blackwater lagoon. I was sure the short trip was worth it when, on my second cast, my large topwater bait generated an explosive strike.

I fought the "fish" to the boat and quickly noticed that I did not have a peacock bass hooked. I had actually hooked two peacocks, one on either end of the Woodchopper. Greg Margerum and Bill Gager entered the same lagoon behind me and noticed my catch. They totaled about five pounds, but made for an interesting start to the day. Greg and Bill moved to the opposite side of the lake and began casting.

Within a couple of minutes, they were hollering. I had my guide motor over for a look. Greg had hooked a giant peacock that immediately dove into a tree. His guide had stripped down and dove in to capture the fish still attached to the hung-up plug. They held up the 13 ½ pound peacock for a couple of photos before releasing it. It was quite an exhilarating experience for all of us.

Unfortunately, the fishing then slowed in that lake and the adjacent one. I moved to another lagoon and found two good fish. The first, a 12 pounder blew up on my topwater worked about 30 feet offshore, and the second, one pushing 14 ½ pounds fell for the same Woodchopper trolled about that distance from the shallow bank. I continued to work other similar waters with depths of five to eight feet that day and connected with another three big fish between 12 and 13 ½ pounds. The "double"

A vid angler Greg Margerum hooked this "teener" which got down into some underwater tree limbs. His guide stripped down and went swimming to capture the big fish.

and five others all over 12 pounds in about 5 hours of fishing made for an active day.

Sighting of toucans, numerous macaws and green parrots that week made the ambiance typically Amazon-enjoyable. We noted the beautiful blue morphos butterflies, the huge "pato" ducks and other birdlike, plus

*L*aydowns on deep-water points in the back of lagoons are almost always good structures to fish. Peacock bass cruise them on a regular basis.

9-foot long caiman and a herd of wild hogs, but the most unusual sighting was a catch by Bill while he was fishing with me. We had motored through a mile-long creek for an hour, pushing and pulling the boat over logs and fallen trees to access perhaps the most beautiful lagoon off the Rio Nhamunda.

A Slithering Strike From Overgrown Shoreline

I had caught 4 nice peacocks and our partner boat with Jerry and Chad Gosselink had taken about 5 from the tiny lake when Bill tossed his large minnow bait toward the overgrown shoreline. He set back on the rod and started winding in his lightweight catch. When the catch had been reeled about half way back to the boat, we both almost fell out as we realized his "catch" was a very poisonous, 4-foot long snake. Neither Bill nor I wanted anything to do with the snake telling the guide to cut the line and let it have the plug.

Giant topwaters are still fair game for an aggressive peacock of any size. Some of the most artistic patterns are "painted" on smaller peacock bass.

The snake was hooked about 8 inches back from its viper-shaped head, one that was trying to sink its fangs into anything it could reach. Still the guide wanted to save the plug and diligently controlled the snake with the paddle until he could grasp it just behind the head. He then freed the plug and tossed the worn out snake into the bushes far from the boat. The snake was one of the few I have ever seen in my many trips to the Amazon region. I'm not sure what kind it was but our guide confirmed that it was indeed very deadly!

The following day, I had a very unusual occurrence that I could not believe. I was trolling a big topwater plug about 30 feet off a heavily-wooded lagoon bank, when a 12 pounder jumped on the lure and headed for the timber along the shore. It went airborne as I put pressure on the fish. The peacock jumped straight up three feet out of the water and

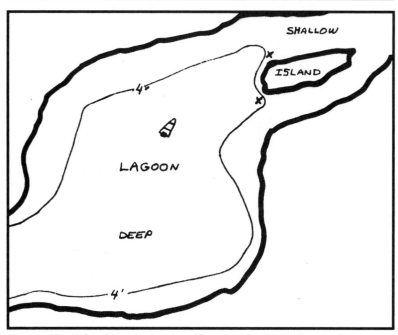

Figure 13 – Islands in the backs of lagoons having adjacent deep water are magnets for the peacocks of the Rio Nhamunda. Most giants will hang out on the points that "touch" depths of 4 feet or more. Shallow flats off the banks seldom harbor giant peacock bass unless they are moving through such an area to feed. Lesson: When after giant peacocks inside dark water lagoons, work topwater plugs over the points of all islands with waters at least 4 feet deep.

slammed into a rotten, 5-inch diameter tree limb. The limb broke and both it and the big peacock came crashing back on the surface. I worked the fish to the boat, expecting it to be knocked out, but it was still very much a fighter. In fact, it didn't show any ill sign of its collision with the deadfall log as I quickly released it.

The Personal Approach To Remote Waters

Our group of 5 anglers was small, and that's a big advantage when you're after pressured peacock bass. The Nexus Explorer is a classic Amazon riverboat that is ideal for taking small fishing parties into remote areas of Brazil. The boat explores the Upper Nhamunda River and

*T*he Nexus houseboat offers perhaps the best staff service of all operations. The accommodations are comfortable and there is plenty of headroom for tall anglers aboard.

other tributaries in search of trophy-class peacocks and giant jungle catfish. It accommodates up to 6 anglers a week, allowing for a more personalized angling adventure by an excellent staff.

That means only three 18-foot long fishing boats will be fishing the area from the Nexus. In waters fairly close to villages, that can be important. On the Lower Nhamunda, there was quite a bit of evidence of netters and commercial fishing boats. To escape them, you have to motor far away either with the Nexus or with the wooden fishing boats. You have to work into difficult-to-reach waters or those protected by the village counsel chiefs or mayors. Nexus owner Reinaldo Jose Tonete has established relationships with some and has purchased rights to sport fish the lagoons under some locals' controls.

On day five, Bill and I took a 3-hour ride to one such lake, Lago Matapea, where, after speaking with the ranch owner who controlled the water, we each had on a big fish. Bill's blew up on a Woodchopper fished near the mouth of the lake. He battled it for about five minutes and slowly worked it near the boat. We clearly saw the 15-pound plus peacock darting away from the boat when it saw us at the same time. As I reached for my bogagrip, Bill pulled the tired fish to the surface. It turned on its side, simply opened its mouth, and the lure popped free.

*P*eacocks of the Nhamunda River are striking in appearance and they are especially fond of submerged timber.

Coming Back From Rejection

The Boynton Beach angler was really dejected. But he was also excited about having on and clearly seeing the largest fish he had ever had to the boat. We worked that immediate area hard for about 5 minutes and then noticed a large fish chasing bait against the shore on the opposite side of the lake mouth. Our guide motored us across the 100-

yard wide expanse, and on my second cast, the same fish exploded on my Woodchopper.

It dove into a large submerged tree on the bottom and immediately became entangled. I kept a taut line as the guide maneuvered to the deadfall. There was no tugging on the other end of my line, but our guide stripped to his undies and slid over the side. He freed my plug, which was hooked to the tree about six feet below the surface. The big peacock had earned its release, but without seeing it, we could only guess at its size. I'm confident that it was a fish in the "teens."

Those two fish battles, within eight minutes of each other, really got Bill excited about landing a giant, and on the following day, he did put a giant aboard for photos. He captured a 15 pounder on his Woodchopper and was one of two extremely happy clients aboard the Nexus that evening. The other was Jerry of Miami and Oro Valley Arizona. He caught and released five peacocks including a 16-pound giant that was fooled on a large plastic minnow bait.

Prime Time For 10-Pounders

The prime fishing season on the Rio Nhamunda is October through March, but the water level can play havoc with the fishing and access to it. High water usually allows the peacocks to swim far back into the forest, while low water prevents the Nexus from covering a lot of water from its initial base in the town of Nhamunda. An 8-day itinerary, allowing for a day of travel coming and going will put you on the water 6 full days.

Overall, the five of us caught 70 fish including about 20 over 10 pounds while fishing three full days and three days of about 4 hours each lure tossing on our recent trip. The limited hours and long runs required to access the better lagoons cut into our numbers. Most of the best spots were 2 ½ to three hours away from the riverboat, which couldn't motor upstream past a huge sandbar in the Nhamunda. The Nexus' 18-foot shallow-draft fishing boats have flat bottoms for very stable stand-up fishing, trolling motors and swivel seats.

Unfortunately, the fishing boats have only 15 hp outboards on them, meaning a relatively slow run upstream to the prospective "bounty". On a couple of days, a few of our party took a 4-hour boat ride to previously unfished waters. Had the Nexus with its modern navigation gear made it upstream past the shallow spot, then the fishing rigs would have been very adequate for the much shorter runs to the lakes and lagoons of the upper Nhamunda. We would have had much longer to fish in generally

The Peacock Bass Special is a relatively small lure that was very successful.

better waters that were further away from the towns (and commercial fishermen) of Nhamunda and Faro City.

Comfort At The Edge Of The Third World

Nhamunda is a poor Brazilian river town with a population of 7,000 people. With just a handful of paved streets and another handful of vehicles, bicycles are the primary means of transportation on land. On the river banks in front of the town are several hundred boats of varying sizes. Behind the town are one of the most beautiful paved landing strips that I've ever seen and an unfinished paved road between it and downtown. Why the road hasn't been finished is unknown, but air charters to this region land on a dirt runway at Faro City, which is adjacent to the town of Nhamunda.

Though lacking some luxuries offered by larger sportfishing operations, you certainly aren't roughing it while aboard the Nexus. Amenities include very comfortable, air-conditioned cabins with bunk beds, two separate but convenient bathrooms and large air-conditioned lounge/dining room. Its dining room serves up excellent meals and tall Americans will definitely appreciate the headroom of the Nexus.

The Nexus houseboat operation is currently fishing the upper Rio Negro area near the small town of Santa Isabel. Reinaldo notes that the area is big and it hold good size and quantities of peacock. Seldom are nets or lots of fishermen sighted, and there is just a small population living at the margin of the river. When the water is not rising, the fishing can be very good, he reports. To find out more about the Nexus Explorer and other great Amazon peacock bass fishing opportunities, contact Scott Swanson at FishQuest!, 3375-B Hwy 76th W., Hiawassee, GA 30546; Phone (888) 891-3474; e-mail: questhook@aol.com or visit their websites at www.fishquest.com and www.peacock-bass.com.

Chapter 11

THE AGUA BOA'S THREE-BAR JACKPOT

Brazilian Bonanza Offers Peacock Bass and Larger Catches!

I lobbed the 6-inch plug toward the deep, dark water just beyond the shallow sand bar in front of the boat. The Magnum Jerk'n Sam splashed down in about five feet of tannin-stained water, and I began a typically effective jerk-pause-jerk retrieve. I had jerked the plug twice before enticing the proverbial explosion under the plug. I leaned back hard on the rod as the giant peacock bass with beefy plug in mouth virtually blasted off for deeper water in the pool 50 feet away.

The fish yanked my heavy-action rod parallel to the water's surface, and my cranked-down drag whined as the peacock headed downstream for the mighty Amazon. My rod, reel and heavy braid held, but the powerful giant destroyed my heavy-duty plug as though it were a small lure. I reeled in the remains of my plug and examined it. My partner, Mark Klein, gasped when he saw the demolished remains.

The rear screw eye with tail spinner was bent over 150 degrees toward the front of the lure. The 3X 4/0 extra strength salt-water size treble attached via heavy-duty split ring to that screw eye had two of its hook points straightened. That's pretty much standard fare when even the plugs meet up with a 20 plus pound peacock bass. On numerous occasions I have had giant fish bend the rear screw eye at least 90 degrees. Such a bending of the screw does loosen the rear hardware critically, and it is unwise to continue using the plug after reshaping the screw and tail spinner.

What was unusual, even for a giant peacock, was the destruction of the screw eye holding the front hook. The 4X 4/0 extra-strength treble

The author has caught over 100 "teeners" from the lagoons of the Agua Boa. A variety of lures entice the big peacocks from the 30 or so lagoons on the tiny river.

was gone along with the 125-pound test split ring. That again is rare but not unheard of. The massive wrench-like jaws of a monster peacock can destroy even the heavy split rings. But, the heavy over-sized screw eye buried in the belly of the hardwood plug was stripped open and pried backwards along the lure's underside, as though it was a "thin" piece of wire.

That experience was my first fish of the day on a return visit to the Rio Agua Boa and its secluded lagoons in the state of Roraima in northern Brazil. I am continually amazed at the power of the peacock bass. I've caught a lot of giant fish of many fresh and saltwater species in my 45 years of fishing all over the world, and none have had the capacity to destroy tackle, including lures, line, rods and reels like the peacock bass. None.

The Agua Boa is a small, very remote blackwater tributary of the Rio Branco in the rain forest near the Equator. This was my fifth trip to these waters, this time with Illinois friends, Mark, Joe Cowan and Bruce

Mark Klein is a big fish man from the upper Midwest who caught giant peacock bass, pirarucu and payara from the lagoons off the Agua Boa.

Redeker. It was late in the dry season and the river waters were very low, leaving alternating strips of shallow sandbars and deep pools along its twisting course. Numerous freshwater stingrays moved along the shallow bottom. They bolted as the boat crept along or was poled over the sand bars. Occasionally, we stepped out of the boat to portage the extremely shallow sand bars, but we kept a close eye on all nearby stingrays.

The productivity of the relatively untapped Agua Boa fishery is impressive. Mark and I went on to catch and release 35 peacock bass that afternoon, although our largest was only 12 pounds. I did accidentally hook an 8-foot "jacare" or caiman on a silver spoon. After five minutes, I had him to the boat twice. My 100 pound test braid was holding true, as was the #18 Pet Spoon, but not surprisingly, my guide, Jose, refused to lip the beast. The spoon affixed to its lower jaw finally flew free of our very big predicament.

Team Approach & Sight Fishing Giant Peacock

The maximum size of our big fish seemed to grow each day, and my favorite lakes of years past were still productive. On day two, my partner Joe and I went to Lago Sierrena. In the shallow river waters, the lake just

J *oe Cohen gets help from guide Jose in landing a 17-pounder from a small lagoon near the lodge.*

off the main river channel took almost 4 hours to reach by boat going upstream. We fished it only for 4 hours and began motoring back at three p.m. to get to the lodge by dark. It was worth the trouble of running aground often, getting out of the boat two or three times in three-inch deep water and dragging the rig over the sandy shallows.

Joe and I used the "team approach" (each of us threw at the other's fish or strikes) and managed four or five doubles including a 25-pound double. Joe caught the 13-pounder on a clown-pattern Woodchopper. We ended the day with 28 peacocks that averaged 10 pounds each. My largest, a 15 pounder, was taken on a large, floating minnow-type lure, while my other "teener", a 14-pound peacock fell for an oversized Magnum Woodchopper topwater plug. Both big fish were in about 6 to 8 feet of water in the middle of the small lagoon.

In the super low waters, Joe and I even got in on some sight-casting to free swimming peacocks. The fish swam along near the surface and were often eager to chase down one of our plugs. Placing a lure within

Bruce Redeker caught several giants from the "resacas" or oxbow lakes off the river. Most of the lakes are less than 16 acres.

4 feet of the swimming peacock would garner a strike at least half the time. Many of the resulting catches were fish in the 10 to 13 pound category. My partner and I reminisced about the very active day on peacock fishing on the long ride back to our lodge that afternoon.

As we snacked on the fresh fried peacock fingers that awaited us when we arrived at the lodge, our friends told their war stories also. Everyone in camp had a productive day, it seems. Some of the 8 other anglers at the lodge fished the river pools and some the other lagoons and "resacas", or oxbow lakes. There are about 20 resacas and lagoons within 20 miles of the lodge, but in low water, it takes time to reach them. Most are between 8 and 16 acres and generally have visibilities of 7 to 10 feet.

Walk-In Lakes Part Of The Topography

Two anglers had walked into three of the 15 land-lock lakes that require a short walk of from two minutes to the closest, to maybe 20 for the most distant. The paths are along well-marked trails through an impressive array of tropical flora, but their fishing was spotty. Their

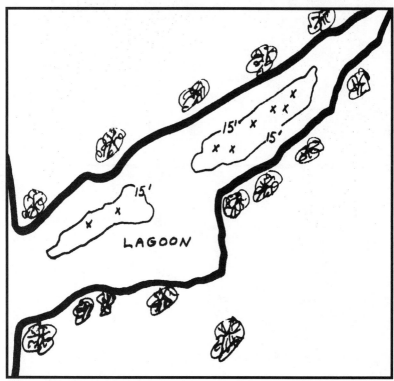

Figure 14 – Some of my favorite lagoons off the Agua Boa are those very deep ones. When waters down the middle are 15 to 18 feet deep and extend several hundred yards, an effective way to catch concentrations of "teeners" is to troll. Giant topwater plugs, spoons and minnowbaits are all productive behind a boat. You can pound the shoreline in such places, but you may miss up to 80 percent of the bounty swimming in the depths of deep-water lagoons. When the bottom topography is variable, use a plug that can be pulled along the entire trolling pass without hanging up. Lesson: After two or more passes without a strike, switch to a different type of bait and continue trolling the depths.

highlights seemed to be the plate-sized orchids of various colors and other air plants that clung to partially-balding trees along the path.

All the anglers in camp commented on the scenery. The Agua Boa and its lagoons are generally surrounded by a variety of hardwoods, including mahogany and palm trees. Bright yellow and orange bushes color the shoreline further. The river headwaters are in the Serra da

This giant male has the huge "spawning hump" on its head, which gives it an even more powerful look. The guides at this operation have vast experience landing such fish.

Mocidade mountain range near the Yanomami Indian Territory southwest of Boa Vista. One can see the mountain peaks that rise to over 6,000 feet, from the fishing grounds north of the lodge.

The lodge is perched on a high riverside bluff beside a picturesque little spring run. It accommodates 10 anglers in double cabanas. A generator placed in the jungle away from the lodge handles the duties of electricity for the stoves, refrigerators, freezers, icemaker, fans, shower heaters and lights. Adjacent the lodge building is a private landing strip carved out of the Amazon Rain Forest for easy air access, even by 20-passenger planes.

River Bars And Pools Strategy

Bruce, an avid tournament bass fisherman from the Chicago area, was my partner for the following three days. His enthusiasm toward the peacock bass was apparent from the first day. Bruce, who with partner Joe had caught two dozen peacocks, landed a 17 pounder. Their guide had pointed out the fish cruising a shallow bar in the river to the twosome. Casts toward the fish drew strikes on each plug, but Bruce's Big Game Woodchopper garnered the hook-up.

"There's two explosions when the big ones hit," laughed Bruce. "One is the peacock, and the other is me."

Not all days on peacock water are joyous however. On day three, Bruce and I managed to lose our three biggest peacocks in a large, deep-water lake about 30 minutes from the lodge where we were staying for the 6 days. We managed a 13-pounder and 17 others averaging about 9 pounds each, but Mark landed two 16-pounders on a giant crankbait while fishing pools in the river with Joe.

Fortunately, the big fish didn't get away the following two days. I landed three 15-pounders in about an hour fishing large, gold minnow baits in Lago Comanda, a few minutes from camp. A mother otter and three youngsters swam along the bank but didn't appear to be disturbed by our fishing. Bruce landed an 18 pound peacock on a large, gold Pet Spoon and I took a 16 ½ pounder on a large, white Luhr-Jensen Pet Spoon from the back of nearby Lago Sappo that afternoon. Two dozen other peacocks averaging 10 pounds each were taken on day four. On the following day, I landed a 19 pounder and another peacock of 15 pounds.

My final day of fishing the waters of the Agua Boa was very eventful. From a lake about three and one half hours (each way) from the lodge, Mark and I caught and released 28 peacocks including several monsters. In the five hours of fishing, we also caught two giant catfish and some other species of fish.

Diving Baits For Small Lakes

The biggest peacock bass of the trip, a 20-pounder hit my gold, diving minnow bait and gave me quite a tussle before we were able to grab it by the lower jaw. The spool of braid on my Abu-Garcia Morrum shrunk to about half its former size as the awesome peacock charged toward the far side of the small lake. The fish finally slowed down and turned as I gained a modicum of control with the baitcaster. After two more spectacular jumps, the fish's heaving gills was a sign it was tiring. My outfit's smooth drag and steady rod pressure brought the big boy to the boat. The fish measured 34 ½ inches long with a girth of 22 inches.

About an hour later I set the hook into another monster. I battled the 16 pounder to the boat where it was weighed, photographed and released. Mark, throwing a huge musky plug, caught two 14-pounders. Together, we added five 12-pounders and 10 others in the 10 and 11 pound category. We figured that we had taken 57 pounds of peacock bass per

Most experienced anglers, like the author, would rather battle giant peacock bass than the stingrays and/or 9-foot long caiman that are also numerous in the Agua Boa watershed.

hour in that one lagoon. That tally didn't include the other fish we landed like Mark's big surprise.

He had cast his huge diving vibrating plug into the depths of the lake and had started his slow crank back when his rod bowed, almost jerking the rod from his hands. "Pirarucu", he yelled, as the fish pulled drag at will. After a five-minute battle we saw what was giving him fits. It was a 40 pound redtail catfish or "pirarara" as its called in Brazil. The upper part of the colorful fish is dark brown; the lower half is yellow and the tail a deep red. This catfish fights like any sport fish and is a handful to battle. I've caught two others in that lake previously on a spoon and a minnow bait, but both were only around 24 pounds.

Grand Slam Of Peacocks & Others

The week's fishing was certainly a successful venture for me. I caught over 100 fish, of which 34 were 10 to 12 pounds and 10 others ranged from 14 to 20 pounds. I caught four types of peacock in the waters of the Agua Boa: the "paca" or speckled, the "acu" (pronounced assu) or grande, the "balinha" (pronounced balleia) or butterfly and the "toua" (pronounced tawah) which is a small peacock with maximum weight of two pounds and one without any side markings - bars, dashes, or rosettes. My partners also did well on big fish, although none broke the 20-pound mark.

Our tally that week also included the drum-like "pescada" (silver croaker), a 75-pound air-breathing pirarucu that Mark hooked on his big crankbait, a bicuda, two Dracula-like payara or "cachorra", the sporty shad-like matrincha, several paiche cashorra (dogfish), several toothsome trieda, several 3-foot long aruana and numerous 2 to 3 ½ pound piranha.

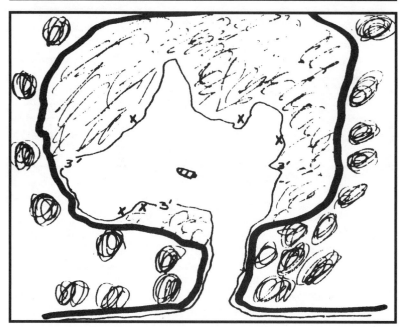

Figure 15 – One of my favorite lagoons in the watershed has about half of it inundated with aquatic vegetation. "Teeners" still exist in the lake, though, for an angler that can fish the 3-foot breakline around the lake. Over about half of it, the submerged grass is on the surface and it helps define that 3-foot breakline. Fish a plug or lure that won't get tangled with grass on ever cast. If you are getting plenty of weeds, you are casting too far into the shallow where few giants exist on this lake and those like it. Lesson: Don't let aquatic weeds hamper your efforts to fool a big peacock. Define the 3-foot depth contour and fish all waters deeper.

Both Mark and I each caught big surubim catfish of around 18 pounds on artificials.

Not all of our time was spent motoring or casting. On three occasions, my guide directed our flat-bottom aluminum boat towards the swampy waters in the back of a small lagoon off the river. He grabbed a machete and moved past me to start whittling at a jungle of vines and brush. A few minutes later, he had cut down enough wood branches to squeeze our craft over a shallow sandbar into a small, undefined creek or cut with additional, but less dense obstacles.

As he whacked off the limbs and vines, I grabbed various tree branches and pushed our boat forward. I marveled at orchids growing in the treetops amidst huge philodendrons whose roots stretched downward like tendrils. My guide cut through the maze of several small trees with huge balls of bugs or "piones" clinging to their bark. The intense exercise in the equatorial sun, although under a partially-shaded canopy of forest, proved to be fruitless on two of our attempts to reach isolated fishing spots. The water had dried up at one locale, and another small lake was just too shallow once we entered it to check on the fishing.

Unusual Sights For "Crocodile Larry"

Green parrots and beautiful yellow macaws flew over us periodically as we "outboard-plowed", paddled and poled our way upstream toward our distant lake. A 400-pound tapir walked out on a sandbar beside us and waded across the river to the other side just 20 yards behind us. We noticed a couple of dozen caiman on the sandbar points and a capybara scrambled along the bank and into the jungle in one section of the river.

Moving along the shallows with the river waters contained well within its banks gave me an opportunity to see some things that I had not seen in some 46 trips to South America. The wild tapir and capybara were just a couple of the unusual sights along the river during daylight hours. I noticed a large, post-spawn peacock swimming out of a deep pool we were slowly motoring through. Closely following the parent as it headed through the adjacent shallow sandy area were over 100 small, 4-inch long fingerlings.

An equally interesting experience occurred as we poled through a long stretch of shallows. Jose, our guide, noticed a 9-foot caiman sliding off the bank into the water. We could see the large reptile move about 20 feet down the bank in the relatively clear river waters, no more than four feet in depth. The "jacare" moved along the bottom and crawled under a fallen tree trunk, six-inches in diameter. It paused its forward movement and lay still under the small branch that crossed over its back. I guess the reptile thought it was sufficiently hidden from us as we approached that spot.

I motioned our guide to pull closer to the massive reptile. My curiosity didn't let me pass up the opportunity to take my push pole and pop him in the back. It felt like running the wooded pole into a brick wall. The caiman exploded out from under the tree branch beside us as I quickly lowered my center of gravity onto the bow pedestal seat, and the caiman headed further downstream toward deeper water. It was just a little more added adventure to our trip to Brazil.

Brazilian Dr. Jan Wilt is the owner of the lodge, which is now named Royal Amazon Lodge. Today, it mostly caters to fly fishermen. With its relatively clear waters, many of the lagoons and the river are ideal for such pursuits! Contact the booking agent(s) for the Royal Amazon Lodge by going to their World Peacock Bass Directory listing at www.peacockbassassociation.com. Much more information on the lodge is available there.

Chapter 12

AMAZON'S ISOLATED XERIUINI RIVER MONSTERS

1,600,000 Areas Of High-Water Biting Peacocks!

It was a typical explosive moment. My lobbed plug hitting the surface of the water seemed to set off the detonation. I leaned back hard on the rod as the giant peacock bass blasted off for the flooded forest... with my eight-inch topwater plug in its mouth.

"Va a media! Va a media!" my friend and fishing operation outfitter Wellington Melo shouted at our guide trying to get him to move the boat quickly to the middle of the lagoon. "Muito rapido! Muito rapido!"

I put as much pressure on the fish, rod, line and reel as I could, as our fishing craft headed away from the trees, but the peacock bass bulled into them. I turned the big fish just in time for it to become entangled in brush at the edge of the flooded jungle. When almost all hope was lost, the fish freed itself of the limbs and swam out of the obstruction.

Albeit somewhat abraded, my heavy 100-pound test line held, as I forced the fish back into open water. The battle was not over yet. Three acrobatic jumps to dislodge the over-sized, 8-inch long Woodchopper topwater and another three powerful runs toward the cover, each time pulling a very tight drag, ensued. I snubbed the fish short of the entanglements again and again, but it did not give up easily. I finally conquered the fish and Wellington grabbed its lower lip with my Boga Grip.

Quick measurements revealed that the 32 inch long peacock weighed 16 ½ pounds and had a 21-inch girth. We took a few pictures, relieved the fire tiger-colored plug from the fish's jaw and released the peacock to fight again. My host, Wellington smiled and reiterated his early morning thoughts about how we would get some big fish close to camp this first day. We were in Lago Cobra just 10 minutes from his operation

A parrot-colored Magnum Woodchopper is deadly on the lagoons off the Xeriuini River. Some 90 lagoons exist along the river.

on the shores of the Xeriuini (pronounced "Sher-e-ou-ni") River in the southwestern part of the Brazilian state of Roraima. The Xeriuini flows southward into the Rio Branco just north of its confluence with the Rio Negro, one of the Amazon River's largest tributaries.

Ninety Lagoons Including The Cemetery

From the Macaroca Lodge, there are 40 named lakes and lagoons downstream and 50 upstream toward the ghost village of Santa Maria. Most of the lakes in the area vary from about 12 to 15 feet deep maximum to some shallower ones that are only 4 to 5 feet. Lago Cobra where I wrestled with the big fish first described lies just downstream from the camp.

Just north of Macaroca in Lago Cementerio (Cemetery), I took a 13-pounder on my first cast to the point at its confluence with the river. I took another 15 between 9 and 12 pounds in that lake and others nearby on one day, including an exciting fish that struck at the boat. I was fishing with a Brazilian helicopter pilot, Cmt. Mauro Rossi, when I noticed that a fish

Beautiful, blackwater lagoons lie just off the river or at the end of oxbow channels from the Xeriuini. Creeks that enter such lagoons may be difficult to traverse, but the extra effort to get through them is usually worth it.

he had brought to the boat had a follower with it. With the lure at my rod tip, I lowered the plug into the water, made three or 4 swishes with lure, and an aggressive peacock of about 10 pounds exploded on it.

That was not the only double we caught. On several other occasions, Mauro and I took two fish at a time, even though the water was slightly high. About 30 percent of our catch over four days was using an effective trolling technique. I would troll a Magnum Woodchopper on my rod while the Brasilia angler would use a 6-inch long Big Game Jerkin' Sam on his. On one pass, I had a 10 pounder smash my plug five times before he was accurate enough for a hook-up. It chased the plug for over 100 feet before getting it!

Wild "Wood" Lake Giants

From the first few casts, Lago Itubal (named after a type of wood) was our most productive lake during the trip. Mauro captured a 15 pounder (31 inch length and 19 ½ inch girth) on the Jerkin' Sam topwater lure. About 20 minutes later, I hooked another giant of 16 pounds that ran into

Wellington Melo is an avid angler who has fished the river and its lagoons more than any other person. This 16-pounder is one of many he has caught.

the trees near the flooded shore and out into the main body before being subdued. The fish measured 31 ½ inches long and had a 20 ½ inch girth.

Two minutes later, Wellington hooked and eventually landed a 13 pounder on a standard size, 6 ¾-inch long Luhr-Jensen Magnum Woodchopper. The following day found us catching additional 13 and 14 pounders and many in the 9 to 12 pound category. Each day, we each caught between 12 and 15 and lost a few of the very largest. We had several other "atocques" or strikes on our topwaters.

On the final day, we ventured upstream toward Santa Maria and beyond fishing the numerous lakes and lagoons. Mauro caught and released a 32-inch long 16 pounder from Lake Peixe Boe and we claimed about 20 others including 10 between 8 and 11 pounds on that short day. Lake Isu produced a couple of big peacocks that pushed 12 pounds each.

*E*ven in moderately high waters, many "teeners" can still be caught in this watershed. Cmt. Mauro Rossi fooled this one with a Big Game Jerkin' Sam topwater plug.

Timing The Quick Releases

Not all action resulted in a successful catch though. One "upper teen" broke my line in open water at Lake Isu, and two similar fish powered their way to the flooded trees and cut my 100-pound test braid. A fourth giant peacock tore the rear hooks from one of my slightly abused Woodchoppers. I saw all of the fish and estimated them to be the 16 to 20 pound category.

Much bigger fish do exist in the area. Wellington notes that he has seen peacock bass weighing 14 kilos, or 29 ¾ pounds, speared by local Indians. In fact, he decided to start his peacock bass operation on the Xeriuini when he saw one that size in the village of Terra Preta. Both Mauro and Wellington have taken 20 pounders from the area.

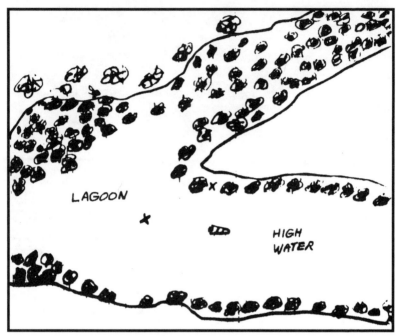

Figure 16 – In high water, big peacocks can still go far back into the trees. Fishing may be off, but there is an approach that sometimes works. Forget about going into the flooded jungle after the fish. Locate hard, high banks and fish along them. The defined banks prohibit the bait and following peacock bass from getting too far away from the main body of the lagoon. If some trees are flooded along the bank and have their trunks in three or 4 feet of water, fish between them. Lesson: When fishing lagoons in high water, hit points and single rows of flooded trees with high banks just behind them. Avoid low water areas where the lagoon has expanded several hundred yards back into the forest!

The best timing for visiting the Xeriuini is in the winter, from November or December through February or March. Waters should be relatively low then, in the dry season and the fishing better than most other spots in the Amazon. Wellington recalls a great January fishing day in which he alone caught and released 45 peacocks and trieda.

There are plenty of botos or freshwater dolphin in the river to view, and a few manatees can be seen on occasion; we saw two on our trip. There were the typical jacare or alligator on some lagoons and colorful

The Macaroca Lodge provides comfortable accommodations in three air-conditioned duplex cabanas with private baths. A restaurant/lounge/dining room is handy to the cabanas.

birds such as macaws, parakeets, kingfishers, heron and patos ducks patrolled the skies above the jungle canopy.

Trophy Tackle Preparation

Most of our big Xeriuini River peacock bass were taken on big Luhr-Jensen topwater plugs, either the Magnum Woodchopper or the Big Game Ripper. Top colors were fire tiger, clown-pattern, and perch. A few peacocks slammed underwater baits, so a well-equipped tackle box should also include a few Tony Acetta #18 Pet Spoons, some one-ounce Krocodile spoons, some large minnow baits, and some heavy duty vibrating plugs.

Straight handle rods that are 6 ½ to 7-foot long and medium heavy action are ideal and a good quality level-wind baitcaster complements the rig. Heavy lines are required for most situations when dense cover is present. Power Pro braided line testing 80-pounds is preferred by many avid peacock bass chasers. The peacock bass is not like any bass you have ever seen, or like any other freshwater fish for that matter. Lighter lines and regular bass lures are easily broken by even the small peacock bass.

Lodging Life And Logistics

The camp has shallow-draft aluminum boats that are 16 feet long with 15 hp outboards, trolling motors and cushioned pedestal seats. In the boat are large coolers with iced drinks and lunch. At the camp are 5 guides, a camp manager, a cook and a laundress/helper. Currently, air conditioned accommodations are provided in three comfortable duplex cabanas at Macaroca. A restaurant/lounge/dining room and a hot water shower house are also handy to the cabanas.

Wellington's partner is Ronaldo Gumiero, a banking consultant from the state capital of Boa Vista about two hours north of the operation. Together, the twosome used aerial observation and contacts with local Indian villages to locate prime fishing waters.

Visitors can access the camp through Manaus, Brazil, the "gateway to the Amazon". The flight from Manaus to Terra Preta aboard a 6-place chartered plane is about 1 ½ hours long, and it is another 45 minutes by boat to Macaroca.

For more information on the Amazon Peacock Bass Fishing Adventure trip, contact Wellington Melo or Ronaldo Gumiero through their website at www.amazonpeacockbass.com or by email at macaroca@osite.com.br, by phone at 011 (55) 959 971-6847 or one of his agents listed on his World Peacock Bass Directory page for Xeriuini Lodge at www.peacockbassassociation.com.

Chapter 13

SANTANA STATUS ON THE MADEIRA

A Captivating Yacht Cruise and Big Catches

"It's now 9:41," I said to my partner, Steve Semesco. "Es tempo para un grande tucunare (It is time for a big peacock)," I told my guide.

Two twitches later, my giant topwater plug was sucked under in a 5-foot diameter implosion on the surface of the water. I set back hard on the rod, as the big fish rocketed away from me. The deep-throated moan from the large casting reel's drag was steady as the fish moved toward one of the numerous trees emerging from the 10-foot deep water.

"Cast to the same place," I shouted to my partner as my fish yanked my rod tip to the surface. I glanced toward my partner to see his rod bowed from an obviously large fish also.

"I'm already hooked up," he laughed. We both had our hands full with the acrobatic fish, as each took to the air. Mine swam around a tree and back out the same way. Guide Natan focused on my fish, the larger of the two, although Steve's 9-pounder was at boatside waiting for netting. A minute later, mine was in the net and so was my partner's.

We quickly weighed the 13-pounder and took pictures of the "double".

"You called that one exactly," Steve acknowledged with a chuckle.

All we needed was some strong sunlight and a productive-looking point in 10 or 11 feet of water. The water on the Rio Matupiri was high and most of the prime spots had an extra 4 to 6 feet of water over them. The flooded trees along what is normally shallows and hard bank were everywhere, but the points were still productive. We moved about 50 yards in the cover off the Matupiri to another point with similar characteristics and put our giant Woodchoppers into the breeze toward our targets.

Mine splashed down about 20 feet away from my partner's, and we began our rhythmic cadence at about the same time. An explosion stopped the "noisy peacock music" and I hung on to a piscatorial freight train. The big fish pulled drag at will, and I struggled to regain control. The Equator's midday heat and humidity were teaming up with the peacock bass to work against me, but I battled on.

Two jumps and 3 more drag-ripping runs from the massive fish were thrilling, and my adrenalin was pumped when I got the big peacock to Natan's waiting net. My guide snared the giant, removed the wooden topwater plug and weighed the fish: 16 pounds! It was a good adjustment for our attitudes that day. Natan leaned over the boat's gunwale to release the fish. As he did, the peacock flipped its broad tail throwing water back in the guide's face. We finished with 20-some fish that afternoon, but no others were "teeners."

High Numbers With Small Lure Tactics

I was able to catch one other teener that week on the Madeira watershed, a 13-pounder, but the big fish bite was slow. Our group of 14 anglers caught about 1500 peacocks, with around 60 over 10 pounds and two 20-pounders. Coloradoan Dave Maynard, host of the Fishing Across America TV show, and 14-year old James Raines of New York City took the big fish honors. Steve Semesco caught a 19-pounder later in the week while fishing the Rio Igapo Acu'. James also captured a 17-pounder from the Rio Tupana as did Gary Tyler of Oklahoma in the Igapo Acu. My 16-pounder, along with a pair of them caught by Ward Foster of Tampa, and another by Gary Tyler, were next in the lineup of big fish.

Rick Schair, owner of Wet-A-Line Tours and host aboard the Santana I yacht "mothership", caught several low to mid-teeners as did Joe Anderson and Jim Campbell. Keith Sutton and Jeff Samsel spent much of their time that week looking for the very elusive catfish but still managed to catch a few large peacocks. Steve Raines and son David, Ed Ray and Bill Toler all caught big peacocks during the week. The overall numbers in each boat were impressive due to lots of schooling action of small fish.

On one day, Jeff and I caught 24 from one school of 2 pounders in 45 minutes on a bay off of Rio Igapo Acu. Jeff caught 9 on a fly. Oklahomans Jim Campbell and Gary Tyler caught 123 peacocks (including two teeners) by concentrating on the schoolies with jigs and other small lures that day. On another day, the twosome caught 129 fish, which included two in the teens. Schools of small fish were very accessible for those wanting to concentrate on them.

*L*arry hoists his 16 pounder that fell for a giant red and white *Woodchopper topwater plug. A few big fish were located in the flooded trees off wooded points.*

Although high water prevailed, the fish were fairly active and the smaller ones were aggressive feeding heavily on schools of sardines. One 3 pound speckled peacock jumped on my plug as it dangled from a tree limb. I set the hook as the fish took off and the limb broke crashing to the water. The line wasn't fouled so it was an easy battle to the boat.

Failed Feeding Fish Approach

On one densely-wooded point we noticed several fish feeding, including a giant that was more than seductive. I tossed my big peacock bass painted surface plug over one tree limb, between and past 3 other pairs of flooded trees to the commotion some 40 yards away. I tried to retrieve it through the gauntlet along the wooded point, but the marauding giant exploded on it leaving a washtub-sized crater. It took off ripping line from the reel as my drag cried for relief. Unfortunately, my line wedged into a fork in the tree branch in front of me that I had cast over. Now I was fighting the tree limb, and the big peacock 30 yards away was trying to make up its mind which flooded brush it wanted to circle three times.

The big fish, with the extra-strength trebles securely impaled, powered away at will in and out of the various flooded timber until it found just the right one to wrap around and break my 80-pound braid. It was all over in less than a minute. I felt helpless with my line wedged in the limb fork just in front of me. My lack of control of that fish resulted in a lost lure and undoubtedly my biggest fish of the trip. My mistake. I didn't have an "exit plan" for when I had hooked the big fish.

After a comfortable overnight flight on Lloyd Aereo Boliviano's 767-300 from Miami to Manaus and a half-hour charter flight onto Autazes, which lies right on the Rio Madeira, we fished the Maderina, the Matupiri, the Igapo Acu and the Tupana Rivers all south of the town. From the air, the area appears to be a huge web of interconnected waterways composed of creeks, islands, oxbow lakes and false river channels galore. In five days, I caught and released around 80 peacocks from countless small coves and points in the four watersheds. The waters on the Tupana were highest during our trip in mid-September making for the toughest fishing in terms of productivity.

Isolation Strategy Equals Big Fish

The secluded Rain Forest waters of the Rio Igapo Acu seemed to be the most productive for us and reportedly the following week's group. The waters farthest away from the area's villages produced the most double-digit giants during both September weeks. The forest surrounds the river and is seemingly impenetrable, but tiny cuts or "igarapies" through the wooded perimeter exist and some lagoons lay at the end of the narrow access.

Traversing into the lagoons was relatively easy at high water, but another 3-foot water level drop would have defined barriers that help

The luxury yacht, Santana I, provided the base of operations for the week probing the tributaries of the Rio Madeira.

limit access to some of the oxbow lakes or "resacas." Most of the flooded trees had about 8 to 10 feet of water beside them during our visit, but during lower water, a visitor would notice that there are laydowns and fallen timber along the banks. There are not as many sandbars on the lower Rio Madeira tributaries as there are along the Rio Negro waterways, but the fish are just as big.

We didn't capture any heavyweight "doubles" but many of us caught two small aggressive peacocks on the same plug. My partner and I had several "partner-doubles", one triple and even a quadruple. On our first cast to a surfacing school of small peacocks, Jeff and I had hookups. I reeled in a pair of fish attached to my giant Woodchopper to a point where our guide could grab the line, and then I picked up another outfit and made a cast, which resulted in an immediate hookup. Jeff reeled in his peacock and I followed suit with our fourth fish. Natan carefully released all four fish.

Grey dolphin and botos (the pink ones) were abundant during our trip. A couple of our boats reported dolphin following their boat as they sought an "easy" meal. Two anglers witnessed a dolphin snatch one of their released fish just five feet away from their boat. As waters continue to recede, they won't be as much of a potential hazard to tired peacocks.

With the waters high, flooded timber was abundant. Some held small fish while other yielded a few giants.

Comfortable Boats And Knowledgeable Guides

Amazon Castaway Tours offers arguably the Amazon's finest luxury fishing yacht currently available, the Santana I, along with excellent fishing platforms, 17 ½ foot long Tracker bass boats with Honda 4-stroke motors, and a stable of the most experienced giant peacock bass guides in South America. The boats have front and rear casting platforms, Lowrance electronics, electric trolling motors and dual batteries, and VHF marine radio's to communicate with the "mother ship". Each boat is supplied with life jackets, first aid kits, hand-held spot lights, emergency flares, large capture nets, scales and basic tool kits.

All of the Santana guides have at least five years guiding experience and most have 10 years or more. Many are related, either as brothers or cousins. They were born and raised in the Amazon watershed of Brazil and are from the various fishing areas. Most of the guides gleaned their knowledge of the vast watershed by venturing out in dugout canoes when they were barely old enough to hold a paddle. As teenagers, they were employed in the commercial aquarium trade. Because of their knowledge of the watershed and their ability to understand changing conditions and fish behavior, they soon became more valuable as sport fishing guides.

The experienced Santana guides are very accommodating. An angler can fish for numbers, chasing after the small schoolies, or he can focus on trophies. He can cast plugs, or flies, or he may troll or even fish with

Outdoor writer Jeff Samsel used his fly rod to work over the schoolies in strong fashion.

live bait if he desires. Several guides are experienced at catching other species such as catfish. Fishing rods in various lengths and actions are furnished on the Santana at no extra charge, which is great for those not wanting to carry a rod box through airports and on various transfers. The Santana also has an ample supply of heavy-duty catfishing rods. They also have an onboard tackle shop and a tackle/reel rental program.

First Class Accommodations/Service

The luxurious Santana I is a 100-foot live-aboard yacht that offers six double-bed suites, each with its own bath, and provides up to 16 fishermen with a level of service and amenities normally associated only with nice hotels. Also available are two master suites containing king size beds and bathrooms. Amenities include, individual air conditioning

The Santana I mothership towed the Bass Tracker boats each evening as we relocated to unfished waters. Up to 16 anglers each week live aboard the yacht and fish from the Trackers.

in all rooms and cabins, washer and dryer, sauna, three separate Jacuzzi baths, room to room telephones, satellite telephone, fax and internet hookups, and in cabin stereo.

The well-staffed Santana I is a safe, comfortable and beautiful home base for your fishing experience. An entertainment room equipped with satellite TV, stereo, DVD, VCR, and gaming table. Electronics include two types of communications radios (VHF & SSB), Lowrance X-15 mapping and GPS system, radar, sonar. The entire ship is appointed in handcrafted mahogany. The beautiful and spacious dining room, upper deck main salon and aft deck open-air bar are favorite gathering places for guests after a day of fishing.

Tasty meals and appetizers of international and regional cuisine are served daily and they include tropical fruits, fresh baked breads, exotic

Amazon fish (such as the fruit eating Tambaqui and the ancient, but delicious - Pirarucu), tender and delicious cuts of Brazilian beef, and regional and international desserts followed by hot Brazilian coffee. There is also an open bar aboard the Santana I and daily laundry service for those who spill their drinks (or want to pack lightly).

For more information on this luxury yacht operation, contact Rick Schair at Wet-A-Line Tours, 5592 Cool Springs Road, Gainesville, Ga. 30506; phone 888-295-4665 or 770-533-9585; fax: 770-533-9587; email: info@wetaline.com or visit their website at www.wetaline.com.

Chapter 14

THE PEACOCK BASS ASSOCIATION

Just When You Thought Books Were Enough!

The Peacock Bass Association (PBA) was formed to unify the world's avid peacock bass anglers, the outfitters and agents that serve them and those companies that offer species-specific products and services. The association promotes the conservation of the peacock bass fishery, including responsible utilization and promotion of the world's greatest freshwater fish, and provides detailed information on the species and how to best catch them. Our comprehensive website, www.peacockbassassociation.com, offers the most complete unbiased information base of booking agents, outfitters, destinations and products and services.

The PBA website is full of extremely useful information for peacock bass anglers. After all, many peacock bass fishing trips cost several thousand dollars, so it's a good investment to learn as much as possible about this fishery in advance of any trip to the Amazon.

Several articles on the PBA website detail specific tactics for peacock bass fishing for novice or experienced anglers. Interesting information on peacock bass, its habits, the various species found throughout South America, the best fishing conditions, and the best timing and pre-planning is also available.

Those anglers who cannot travel overseas might want to know about the peacock bass fishing available in South Florida, and the PBA website has excellent information on where, when and how to plan a trip to this location. Maps, provided by the Florida Fish and Wildlife Conservation Commission, outline the various waterways and ramps for this sometimes elusive fish. Guides, highly recommended, are also listed in the Directory.

This colorful PBA decal quickly identifies your rod case, tackle box, boat and luggage.

World Peacock Bass Directory

The Directory includes all the major players in the industry - site operations, booking agents, outfitters, industry manufacturers and companies that offer peacock bass anglers the best trips, tackle and services. This is the most authentic, up-to-date source that all peacock bass anglers utilize to research the available trips to the world's peacock bass fisheries.

The information is provided in a simple, standard format so that anglers can quickly get an idea of each destination, product or service. A summary of the waters fished, the trip cost, the number of fishing days, and booking agents is included. Websites addresses, e mails and phone numbers provide multiple ways to contact each company.

More than 50 peacock bass operations and product manufacturers/ services are supporting members of PBA. A full contact list is provided to quickly review your options for booking any of your fishing travel needs. See Appendix I for the current PBA Contact List at the time of this writing.

While non-members of PBA can view the directory listing, only members receive a critical benefit of PBA membership - the e-zine/newsletter.

Most peacock bass anglers attribute their success to the information received from the Peacock Bass Association. Individual members know the value of planning in advance of any trip to the Amazon.

"The World of Peacock Bass" Newsletter/eZine

Timely, exclusive and hard-hitting, this newsletter/eZine is distributed 10 times a year only to our members via e-mail. U.S. members without an e-mail address may receive the newsletter by U.S. mail. It is not available to non-members on the website, however, you can register as a guest on the www.peacockbassassociation.com website and receive a one-time free sample. The newsletter/eZine is the only way to learn about the latest peacock bass information throughout the world.

Topics include Member Comments, "insider" news from around the world, new trip offerings, new lures and tackle, outfitter changes, important lure modifications, productive tactics at each location, species information from peacock fisheries biologists and much more by Larry Larsen and other avid peacock bass chasers.

Experiences, both good and bad, from our numerous membership base is shared in the eZine/newsletter with all members. That way, you can get first-person information from other anglers like yourself. These non-

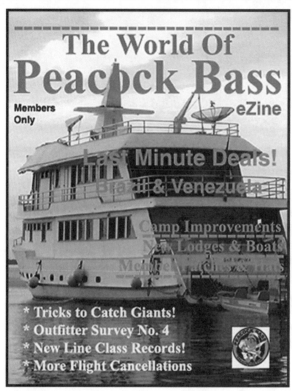

*A*mong the information included in the Peacock Bass Association web magazine are articles on operator surveys, new products, secret tactics, news of the operations and product changes.

commercial tips, topics and tactics of interest have more than paid for themselves numerous times, according to many PBA members.

In addition, important State Department safety warnings or health issues often overlooked by most travelers are issued immediately by e-mail after PBA verifies the significance and impact of any travel or health-related information.

Last Minute Deals On Trips - When last-minute cancellations occur, PBA's Agents and Outfitters may have premium space available to offer at substantial savings to PBA individual members. Anglers can save from $500 to over $1,000 on these last-minute deals offered by Supporting Members if you can go on relatively short notice. These last-minute deals are only offered in our members-only newsletter/eZine.

Other Membership Benefits

Personal Consultation - Larry's phone rings constantly with calls from new and experienced peacock bass anglers who want to "pick his

The Peacock Bass Association brings together avid anglers, agents and outfitters and those offering products and services to the industry. Our focus is to promote fishery conservation, communication and knowledge of this sport.

brain" on a particular destination or a situation. New members automatically receive one free 5-minute telephone consultation with Larry, an invaluable personal resource that could save you hundreds of dollars on your next trip.

Member Photo Gallery - Show off your favorite catch and see the excitement of other members' trips in a selection of photos which are continuously being updated. Rather than sending a photo of your trophy catch to each friend, just direct them to the photo gallery where your photo will appear with other PBA members who are proud to display the largest fish of their trip.

Books and Merchandise Discounts - PBA members receive additional discounts off our many Peacock Bass books and other products. Specialized Peacock Bass merchandise includes a very informative video, T-shirts, PBA patches, PBA hats and very attractive limited edition prints of various peacock bass species. Colorful PBA decals quickly identify your rod cases, tackle boxes, luggage and boats. Additional discount offers from Supporting Members of PBA are also available only to members.

Memberships

PBA offers Standard, Premium and 3-Year memberships. Some membership levels include premium items such as books, T-Shirts and/or hats. The most updated information is available at the PBA website - www.peacockbassassociation.com. Individuals may sign up with a check, money order or credit card by completing the Membership Form. All individual member information is confidential and is not shared with anyone outside of PBA.

Agents, outfitters and companies which offer a destination, product or service to peacock bass anglers are welcome to review the Supporting Membership information.

www.peacockbassassociation.com

Isn't it time you reviewed this website? Check out the variety of membership options/benefits available and call with any questions.

APPENDICES

APPENDIX I
World Peacock Bass Directory Contact Listing

APPENDIX II
"Peacock Bass Explosions" Contents

"Peacock Bass & Other Fierce Exotics" Contents

"Peacock Bass Addiction" Contents

APPENDIX III
Peacock Bass Resource Directory

APPENDIX I

Following is an alphabetical list of those companies that book peacock bass trips or sell products and services specifically designed for this fishery. They are the top travel, product and service companies in their field. Many agents also book trips to Alaska, Central America, the Caribbean and beyond, so check with them on all your international outdoors travel needs. The industry listed also offer products and services applicable to many other species, including domestic. Check out their websites for full details and tell them you were referred by the Peacock Bass Association.

Acute Angling,
P O Box 18, Califon, N.J. 07830 USA
Phone (908)832-2987 FAX (908)832-2989
e mail - preiss@acuteangling.com
website - www.acuteangling.com

Aimbar
Phone - 011-5844-22 06 49
and 011-5844-21 57 52
e mail - aimbar@telcel.net.ve
website - www.aimbar.com

Alan Zaremba Guide Service,
1604 North Park Road,
Hollywood, FL 33021
Phone (954)961-0877
e mail - SFLPEACOCK@aol.com

Amazon Angling Adventures Ltd,
6915 Hudson Village Creek Rd.,
Kennedale, TX 76060
Phone 817-483-8880   Fax: 817-483-8644
e mail: ronjr@amazonpeacock.com
website: www.peacockbassanglers.com

Amazon Fishing Planners,
P.O. Box 2533, Agencia Central, Manaus,
Amazonas 69001-970 Brazil
Phone 011-55-92-9124-1206
FAX 011-55-92-223-1333
e mail - amazonfishingplanner@hotmail.com
website - www.peacockbass.com.br

Amazon Peacock Bass Fishing Adventure
 Boa Vista, Roraima, Brazil
Phone 011-55-95 9971-6847
e mail - macaroca@osite.com.br
website - www.amazonpeacockbass.com

Amazon Tours,
751 Canyon Dr., Suite 110,
Coppell, TX 75019 U.S.A. -
Phone (888)235-3874
FAX (972)304-5262
e mail - usa@peacockbassfishing.com
website - www.peacockbassfishing.com

Andetur USA LLC/Natour,
 P O Box 52, 105 Old Oak Dr.,
Montegut, LA 70377
Phone (866)798-6029
 FAX (985)250-5298
e mail - dreid@andetur.com
website - www.aracacamp.com

B & B World Wide Fishing Adventures,
1416 1/2 East 10th Place,
The Dalles, OR 97058
Phone (888)479-2277
FAX (541)296-9144
e mail - getfishing@wheretofish.com
website - www.wheretofish.com

Bassmex, 2809 Sheldon St.,
Clovis, NM 88101 USA
Phone (888)769-0220;
FAX (505)769-0051
e mail - bill@bassmex.com
website - www.bassmex.com

Desarrollos Turisticos Uraima C.A
(Peacock Bass Lodge),
Calle Geminis c/c Av Atlantico
Edif. Hazerot Suites, Valencia, Venezuela
Phone (011)58-241-6-714-6006
e mail - hlmc@icnet.com.ve
website - www.pavonpayara.com

The Detail Company,
3220 Audley, Houston, TX 77098 U.S.A.
Phone (800)292-2213
FAX (713)524-7244
e mail - dove524@detailco.com

Explorations Inc.,
27655 Kent Rd.,
Bonita Springs, FL 34135 U.S.A.
Phone: (800)446-9660
FAX (941)992-7666
e mail - cesxplor@aol.com
website - www.goexploring.com   /

FishQuest!,
Fieldstone Marina
3375-B Highway 76 W,
Hiawassee, GA 30546 USA
Phone (888)891-3474;
FAX (706)896-1467
e mail - questhook@aol.com
website - www.fishquest.com;
www.peacock-bass.com

Fishabout,
P.O. Box 1679,
Los Gatos, CA 95031 U.S.A.
Phone (800)409-2000
FAX (408)395-4676
e mail - trips@fishabout.com
website - www.fishabout.com

Fishing with Larry (Larry Schoenborn)
14312 SE 22nd Circle,
Vancouver, WA 98683-8421
Phone (800)205-3474
FAX (360)896-4755
e mail - fish@fishingwithlarry.com
website - www.fishingwithlarry.com

Hawghunter Guide Service
1000 N State Road 7,
Hollywood, FL 33021
Phone (954)325-1115
FAX (954)986-6999
e mail - cobby12345@aol.com
website:www.hawghunterguideservice.com

High Hook Fishing Tours
(Belo Monte Fishing Lodge)
Rua Teofilo Otoni, 135-401 Centro,
Rio de Janeiro 20090-080, Brazil
Phone - 011-55-21-2516-9622
FAX 011-55-21-2516-7714
e mail - highhook@transpacific.com.br
website - www.fishinginamazon.com

Jim Conley's Outdoors Adventures,
606 Pinar Dr., Orlando, FL 32825
Phone (407)249-1387
FAX (407)249-1387
e mail - conleyjn@aol.com

Menno Travel Service,
4111 Central Ave. N.E., Suite 107,
Minneapolis, MN 55421 U.S.A.
Phone (800)635-2032 or (763) 788-6288
FAX (763)788-2536
e mail - pauls@mennotravelservice.com
website - www.junglesedgetours.com

Nexus Explorer
email - nexus@argo.com.br
Peacock Princess, 1910 NW 97th Ave.,
Miami, FL 33172
Phone (011)-58-414-322-3708; FAX 212-264-6875
e mail - ga@peacockbassprincess.com
website - www.peacockbassprincess.com

Peacock Bass South,
10142 Culpepper Ct., Orlando, FL 32836
Phone (407)363-0009 FAX (407)363-0033
e mail - pkbasssouth@aol.com

Peacock Bass Trips.com,
476 Cameron Drive, Weston, FL 33326
Phone (859)221-6360; FAX (859)269-6360
e mail - peacockbasstrips@bellsouth.net
website - www.peacockbasstrips.com

Reel It Up LLC,
2921 Christopher Court,
Birmingham, AL 35243 USA
Phone toll free (866)801-3209; (205)970-0152; FAX (205)968-7331
e mail - Reelitup@hotmail.com
website - www.reelitup.com

River Plate Anglers
e mail - anarpa@adinet.com.uy
website - www.riverplateanglers.com

Rod & Gun Resources, Inc.,
206 Ranch House Road, Kerrville, TX
78028 U.S.A.
Phone: (800)211-4753
FAX (830)792-6807
e mail - venture@rodgunresources.com
website - www.rodgunresources.com

Ron Speed's Adventures,
1013 Country Lane,
Malakoff, TX 75148
Phone 903-489-1656;
FAX 903-489-2856
e mail - ron@ronspeedadventures.com
website - www.ronspeedadventures.com

Sportfishing Worldwide,
9403 Kenwood Rd., Suite C-110,
Cincinnati, OH 45242 USA
Phone (800)638-7405
FAX (513)891-0013
e mail - info@sfww.com
website - www.sfww.com

Trek International Safaris,
P.O. Box 1305, Ponte Vedra, FL
32004-1305 U.S.A.
Phone (800)654-9915 FAX
(904)273-0096
e mail - trek@treksafaris.com
website - www.treksafaris.com

Unini River Fishing Adventure,
Boa Vista, Roraima, Brazil
Phone/FAX 011-55-95-624-1664
e mail - unini@technet.com.br
website - www. uninifishing.com

Wet-A-Line Tours,
5592 Cool Springs Road, Gainesville,
GA 30506, USA
Phone (888)295-4665
FAX (770)533-9587
e mail - rwschair@america.net
website - www.wetaline.com

Wilderness Adventures,
5040 Highlands Rd.,
Franklin, NC 28734
Phone (828)524-3677
FAX (828)349-4200
e mail - fuchs@dnet.net
website - www.wildernesstaxidermy.com

World Wide Angling Adventures,
515 Trailside Court, Roswell, GA 30075 USA
Phone - 770-998-0487
Fax - 770-998-3274
e mail AmazonVoyager@aol.com
website - www.AmazonVoyager.com

Industry Products/Services

BogaGrip (available through QuesTackle)

The Fishing Connection Lure Company,
P O Box 18, Gordonville, MO 63752
Phone (573)243-3074
e mail - jkaempfer@clas.net

G. Loomis, Inc.,
1359 Down River Drive,
Woodland, WA 98674 U.S.A.
Phone (800)662-8818 FAX (360)225-7169
e mail - bholt@gloomis.com
website - www.gloomis.com

Great Fish Reproduction Studio,
P.O. Box 940, Bolivar, MO 65613, USA;
Phone (866)424-7834 FAX 417-326-3443
e-mail: info@4greatfish.com
website: www.4greatfish.com

Luhr-Jensen & Sons Inc.,
400 Portway Ave.,
P O Box 297, Hood River, OR 97031
Phone (800)535-1711;
Outside USA (541)386-3811
e mail - custserve@luhrjensen.com
website - www.luhrjensen.com

Plano Molding Co.,
431 E. South St., Plano, IL 60545 USA
Phone (800) 226-9868, FAX (630)552-8989
Email – customercare@planomolding.com
Website – www.planomolding.com

Power Pro (available through QuesTackle)

Questackle,
Fieldstone Marina
3375-B Highway 76 W,
Hiawassee, GA 30546 USA
Phone (888)891-3474;
FAX (706)896-1467
e mail - questhook@aol.com
website - www.fishquest.com;
www.peacock-bass.com

**Rufus Wakeman Peacock Bass Fly
Fishing Tournament,**
2325 N. E. Indian River Drive, Jensen
Beach, Florida, 34957
Toll Free (800) 305-0511; Phone (772)
334-4645 Fax (772) 334-6075
e mail - HTTNA@aol.com
website - www.peacockbasstournament.com

Stamina Inc,
P.O. Box 26745, Minneapolis, MN 55426
Phone: 952-926-1994; Fax: 952-926-2084
Toll Free Order Line: 800-546-8922
e mail - info@staminainc.com
website - www.staminainc.com

Tackle-Box.net,
9 Powelson Dr.,
Hillsborough, N.J. 08844 USA
Toll free (866)431-1668
FAX (908)832-2989
e mail - greiss@rcn.com
website - www.Tackle-box.net

TTI Companies-Daiichi Hooks,
P O Box 1177, Wetumpka, AL 36092
Phone (800)774-6657
 FAX (334)567-9788
e mail - info@tticompanies.com
website - www.daiichihooks.com

APPENDIX II

"Peacock Bass Explosions" Contents

Part 2. Preparing For Action

11. TOP TACTICS FOR TROPHIES
Trolling, school activating and other productive methods
Typical Haunts
Top Submergent and Surface Methods
Speed Trolling
School Activations
More Giant Doubles
Minnow-Bait Comeback

12. TACKLE FOR THE FRESHWATER BULLY
Here are the keys to productive lure selection
Topwater Plugs
Minnow Plugs
Searching The Depths
Jigs and Vibrating Plugs
Spoons and Spinners
Attention to Detail
Appropriate Tackle

13. FLYFISHING EXCITEMENT
Peacocks love to feed on the surface
Fly Class Records
Wading Action
Streamers and Poppers
Colors and Patterns
Cast-and-Retrieve Tactics
Outfitting For Location
Leader and Tippet Thoughts
Rod Weights
Stripping School

14. BOAT-SIDE BATTLES
The world's most explosive freshwater fish
Guide Overboard Maneuvers
Dumb, Mean and Powerful
Contact and Initial Run
Fight To Exhaustion

15. BIOLOGY AND LIFESTYLE
Behaviors are becoming to this brute
Sexual Maturity
Pre-Spawn Behavior
Spawning Behavior
Post-Spawn Behavior
Shared Parental Care
Juvenile Growth
Adult Growth
Foraging Preferences
Bass Feeding Comparisons
Foreign Competition
Survival of The Fittest

16. TRAVEL TIPS/REQUIREMENTS
Health, Timing, Equipment and Expectations
Travel Requirements/Options
Health Precautions
Clothing and Personal Items
Packing Tips and Tricks
Timing Your Venture
The Right Equipment For Handling Peacocks
Other Fishing Tackle You'll Need
The Guides, Language And Tipping

"Peacock Bass & Other Fierce Exotics" Contents
INTRODUCTION - THE FIERCE EXOTICS ON TRIAL

"Peacock Bass Addiction" Contents

INTRODUCTION - PEACOCK BASS ADDICTION

7. PERUVIAN TREASURES
Exploring the Amazon headwaters for eco-enjoyment
Maranon Missions
Tiger Tracks
Napo Cochas
Yavari Yarns
Timing The Bite
Night Nature Walks/Other Interests

8. THE MYSTERIOUS XINGU
Golden peacocks swim with giant crocodile perch and other exotics
Fifth World Peacocks
Multi-Specie Strikes
Frontier Settlement Selection
"The Land Where No One Walks"
A Blastin' Good Time

9. VENEZUELA'S RANCH LAND LAKES
The fish bully's on the ranch are in the flooded forests
Timber Testimony
Prime Lunker Habitat
Birthday Bass
Time-Limited Action

10. WORLDLY LOCATIONS FOR ACTION
Spanning the globe for some additional highs
Florida Peacocks Up Close
Hawaii's Hula Peacock
Lago Balbina and Rio Tupana
Other Brazilian Discoveries
Venezuela's Pasimoni Activity
Lake Guri Hangs On

11. TUCURUI AND OTHER NORTHEAST BRAZIL HOTSPOTS
The many productive peacock waters in the State of Para
Tournament Time
Stressing Catch-And-Release
Pristine Para State
Tucurui & Tributaries
Central Amazon Lakes Region
Tapajos/Trombetas Tributes

12. MATO GROSSO GOLD
Chasing the elusive golden dorado in the Great Swamp
Piraputanga Passions
Golden Gospel
Peacock Possibilities
Water, Water, Everywhere
World's Biggest Ecological Sanctuary
World's Largest Tournament

APPENDIX III

YOU'VE INVESTED THOUSANDS OF DOLLARS ON YOUR TRIP, NOW LEARN HOW TO MAKE IT MOST SUCCESSFUL!

Larry's books on peacock bass fishing are dedicated to those anglers who are interested in tangling with the most exciting fish of their lives. The books are filled with invaluable information that even expert anglers will find helpful. What you will learn from Larry's numerous trips to South America will make your trip more productive and more enjoyable!

PF1 - PEACOCK BASS EXPLOSIONS! details when, where and how to catch America's greatest gamefish! Top tactics from around the world help you catch more and larger peacocks. This informative, comprehensive reference book with numerous photos and maps is invaluable to all adventurous anglers with a yearning to battle the explosive peacock bass!

PF2 - PEACOCK BASS & OTHER FIERCE EXOTICS covers the exciting peacock bass and other freshwater species of Latin America. The detailed book reveals the very latest techniques, lures, and patterns that fool the provocative fish, along with over 80 informative illustrations and photos. While the majority of strategies are focused on peacock bass, proven tactics for the "river draculas," called payara, and other exotics are discussed in detail.

PF3 - PEACOCK BASS ADDICTION! offers tips on where and how to catch this exciting fish, including range/seasonal movements, fly fishing tips, battle tips and comprehensive tackle and equipment recommendations. The latest information to prepare you for the ultimate experience, along with 12 steps to "survive" the jubilation and ecstasy are revealed.

PF4 - AMAZON PEACOCK BASS FISHING! - TOP TACTICS FOR TOP LOCATIONS outlines many of the most productive and enjoyable destinations in South America which have consistently produced large numbers of peacock bass as well as peacock bass over 10 pounds. Numerous first-person anecdotes will provide novice and experienced peacock bass anglers with interesting hard-to-believe actual experiences of catching "teeners" in the Amazon.

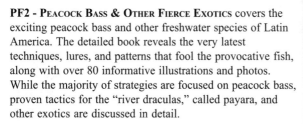

VID-2 - MASTERS' SECRETS OF PEACOCK BASS FISHING - a comprehensive video with exciting footage and excellent tips and tactics on where and how to catch South America's most exciting freshwater fish. Forty secrets are revealed for catching bigger peacock bass and more of them. You will learn how to determine the most effective presentation to locate and catch "teeners." The author guarantees you will learn new tactics for catching bigger peacock! A great item to complement any library on peacock bass fishing.

COMING SOON!

QUALITY T-SHIRTS AND HAT

Striking all-cotton T-shirts feature the same beautiful paintings that appear on the cover of *"Peacock Bass Explosions"* or *"Peacock Bass Addictions."* Show off your involvement in America's greatest freshwater gamefish. Your choice of *Peacock Bass Explosions* **(TS1)** *or Peacock Bass Addictions* **(TS2)**, these quality white shirts with four-color art on their front can be ordered in a variety of sizes. See order form for details.

H1 - Attractive mesh baseball cap with Peacock Bass Patch prominently displayed - cap is white with black visor. Adjustable to all sizes. Available to PBA members only.

FULL COLOR LIMITED EDITION PRINTS

Individually numbered and personally signed by the artist, these foam core-mounted prints are available while supplies last. This collector's item is suitable for framing and makes a handsome addition to any room in the home or office.

LEP-1 - Beautiful painting of the seven peacock bass species with their unique color variations; profiles by renown marine watercolorist Beverly Thomas. Available in 11" x 11" size.

LEP-2 - An exciting painting of peacock bass feeding on a piranha by accomplished angler and artist George Liska, available in 11" x 14" size.

TRANSLATION SHEETS & GIANT PEACOCK WEIGHT COMPUTER

The 8½" x 11" laminated English/Portuguese (T/C1P) & English/ Spanish (T/C2S) Vocabulary Translation Sheets make communication easier with non-English speaking guides. On the back of the laminated sheets is Larry's Giant Peacock Weight Computer. By using a tape to record the length and girth of the fish, you will know immediately the weight of the fish you've just landed. This has been proven to be the most accurate method of determining weights of giant peacock without a certified scale!

Index

LARSEN'S OUTDOOR PUBLISHING

WWW.LARSENOUTDOORS.COM

ALL PRICES INCLUDE POSTAGE/HANDLING

FRESH WATER

___ BSL3. Bass Pro Strategies ($14.95)

___ BSL6. Bass Fishing Facts ($13.95)

___ BSL8. Bass Patterns ($14.95)

___ BSL9. Bass Guide Tips ($14.95)

___ CF1. Mstrs' Scrts/Crappie Fshg ($12.95)

___ CF2.Crappie Tactics ($12.95)

___ CF3.Mstr's Secrets of Catfishing ($12.95)

___ LB1. Larsen on Bass Tactics ($15.95)

SALT WATER

___ IL1. The Snook Book ($14.95)

___ IL2. The Redfish Book ($14.95)

___ IL3. The Tarpon Book ($14.95)

___ IL4. The Trout Book ($14.95)

___ SW1.The Reef Fishing Book ($16.45)

___ SW2.Masters Bk/Snook ($16.45)

PEACOCK BASS

___ PF1.Peacock Bass Explosions! ($17.95)

___ PF2.Peacock Bass & FierceExotics ($17.95)

___ PF3.Peacock Bass Addiction ($18.95)

___ PF4 Amazon Peacock Bass Fishing ($19.95)

___ VID-2 Masters' Secrets of Peacock Bass

Fishing (approx 50-min. video) ($29.95)

(AVAILABLE SOON)

REGIONAL

___ FG1.Secret Spots-Tampa Bay/
Cedar Key ($15.95)

___ FG2.Secret Spots - SW Florida ($15.95)

___ BW2. Guide/Cntral Fl.Waters ($15.95)

___ BW3.Guide/South Fl.Waters ($15.95)

___ OT3. Fish/Dive Florida/ Keys ($13.95)

HUNTING

___ DH1. Mstrs' Secrets/ Deer Hunting ($14.95)

___ DH2. Science of Deer Hunting ($14.95)

___ DH3.Mstrs' Secrets/Bowhunting ($12.45)

___ TH1. Mstrs' Secrets/ Turkey Hunting ($14.95)

OTHER OUTDOORS BOOKS

___ DL2.Manatees/Vanishing Mermaids ($11.45

___ DL3.Sea Turtles/Watchers'Guide ($11.45)

___ DL4 If I Were a Manatee - A Coloring and
Activities Book ($4.95)

INTERNATIONAL AIRMAIL ORDERS
Send check in U.S. funds; add $7more
for 1 book, $5 for each additional book

BIG MULTI-BOOK DISCOUNT!
2-3 books, SAVE 10%
4 or more books, SAVE 20%

ALL PRICES INCLUDE U.S. POSTAGE/HANDLING

No. of books _____ *x $* _____ *ea =* $ _____

No. of books _____ *x $* _____ *ea =* $ _____

Multi-book Discount (%) $ _____

SUBTOTAL $ _____

Priority Mail
(add $3.00 for first book and $2 for each additional book) $ _____
☐ **TOTAL   ENCLOSED   (check or money order) $** _____

NAME _____ *ADDRESS* _____

CITY _____ *STATE* _____ *ZIP* _____

Credit card orders - Order on www.larsenoutdoors.com or send check/
Money Order to: Larsen's Outdoor Publishing,
Dept. PF4, 2640 Elizabeth Place, Lakeland, FL 33813